D1602904

FOREVER HOME...

DOG TRAINING 101 & HOW TO BE A BETTER SHELTER VOLUNTEER

MIKE DEATHE CPDT-KA

PUBLISHED BY FASTPENCIL

Published by FastPencil
307 Orchard City Drive
Suite 210
Campbell CA 95008 USA
info@fastpencil.com
(408) 540-7571
(408) 540-7572 (Fax)
http://www.fastpencil.com

This book is for educational purposes only. You should always have a professional dog trainer present whenever these or other techniques are being implemented. Do not institute these ideas in your shelter without consulting the staff and management.

Printed in the United States of America.

First Edition

This book is dedicated to those dogs that never made it out alive… For the memory of them and the sake of those still in shelters, lets get out there and make a difference!

❧

ACKNOWLEDGMENTS

I know I will forget someone here so I apologize up front, but thank you to:

Kate for helping me with the edits.

Humane Society of Greater Kansas City, for edits and allowing me to be part of the team.

KC Pet Project, for edits and letting me help from time to time.

Animal Haven for starting this idea many years ago with a simple talk to the volunteers.

Contents

INTRODUCTION

To start this book in the most logical way, I need to introduce myself. My name is Mike Deathe. I am a dog trainer from Shawnee, KS with a BA in Psychology from KU; a professional member of the Association of Pet Dog Trainers; and an American Kennel Club Canine Good Citizen Evaluator. I volunteer with several animal shelters in the Kansas City Metro, and have seen first-hand the effect of shelter life on dogs and dog behavior. This is the primary reason for writing this book. While there never seems to be enough prospective pet owners to save all the dogs in shelters, there seems to be, at least in KC, no shortage of people who want to help and to become volunteers. That's the good news! The bad news is...most of the folks who want to help have little, if any, experience of how to train a dog, and nominal understanding of dog behavior in general. In many cases, good hearted, well intending people actually do more damage to shelter dogs than help them, because of that lack of knowledge.

About a year ago I was asked by a local shelter to put together a presentation for their volunteers that covered dog training basics, canine body language and my thoughts of what volunteers should actually be doing with dogs in a shelter. After many presentations and supplemental clinics, I realized that a book needed to be written on this topic. While this book may not ever be a best seller, I feel it is way overdue. Additionally, while its goal is to improve the shelter world, it will no doubt also help folks with their own dogs at home; and isn't that the end goal? Hell, I have even put video highlights from the presentations up on our Kiss Dog Training website to help those who don't like to read! I could really care less how the information gets out there, all I know is it needs to spread like wildfire!

My goal in writing this book is to give volunteers (and pet owners) three things:

1. A basic understanding of positive reinforcement dog training.
2. An introduction to the three types of volunteers I believe every shelter needs.
3. A basic primer in dog body language, and how to stay safe in a shelter   environment.

According to the Humane Society of the United States, in 2010 alone, 6-8 million pets (dogs and cats) entered animal shelters and only 3-4 million were adopted. You do the math, but my calculations say that those other 3-4 million animals die in shelters each year. I can tell you from personal experience as a dog trainer that many of those dogs ended up in shelters due to behavioral issues. As you read this book, you will hopefully see that if we implement some, if not all, of the ideas found here, volunteers across America will be able to actively take part in making dogs more adoptable, thus helping them find their forever homes. Let's face it people, isn't that why we allow dogs into our homes as foster parents, or adoptees or the reason for becoming shelter volunteers?

A final note on this book: I have never, nor will I ever claim to know everything about dogs or dog training. I have no doubt there will be some people who might disagree with my ideas and/or the messages in this book. I simply ask you to read the book, keep an open mind, take only what you like, and leave the rest right here in these pages. My goal is that you love the entire book, but if not, I hope you find something you can use at your local animal shelter or at home with your own dog. It just might be the difference between a dog running out of time and a dog learning the skills that will help him find his forever home! Enjoy the book, get out there, make a difference, and be a better volunteer!

1

THE FUTURE IS THE PAST...

Let's say you had a time machine, traveled back 20 to 30 years and decided to stop in at the local animal shelter to look at the dogs and cats. It would be very different than the shelters you see today. This difference is in the make-up of the population of the shelter. We have done such a good job with one problem that we have inadvertently created another one. Years ago it was determined (correctly) that overpopulation was the main problem in shelters. Very few dogs were getting "fixed" and the population of puppies was exploding. When you walked into a shelter back then, there were usually more puppies than dogs of any other age. Even though puppies are cuter and more adoptable, there were just too many of the furry little critters to find homes for all of them. The solution that took shape was with the idea of spay and neuter programs; where as a rule, every shelter dog was fixed. With lots of hard work and education about the importance and benefits of "fixing" animals, we witnessed not only a decrease in the number of puppies but also the creation of low-cost spay and neuter programs all over the country...we made a difference.

Today the number of puppies in shelters has decreased dramatically, which is great, but now we find ourselves in a world where the majority of shelter dogs are of the juvenile/adolescent variety. Unfortunately, these dogs are typically not as cute, needy, or emotionally pleasing as their puppy counterparts, which makes them much harder to adopt. On top of all of this, many shelter dogs now come to the shelter by owner surrender or from being picked up by animal control because they got out and nobody went looking for them. Ask yourself two simple questions...

1. Why would someone get rid of a perfectly good dog?
2. Why are the majority of these dogs between the ages of 6 months and 18 months?

The answer is two-fold: lack of appropriate training combined with a difficult developmental period, otherwise known as PROBLEM BEHAVIORS. People today find it easier to take a dog to the pound and drop it off, rather than putting in the work to prevent the problems. With this book, my hope is that we as volunteers and even some of the folks at home, can do what the volunteers of the past did. With hard work and education on dog training dog behavior, we can make a difference; thus learning how to prevent and/or fix these problems. We, as pet owners and volunteers, must take the first step, and pay attention to how we react to the dogs around us in a shelter environment and/or at home.

2

LOVE BLIND!!!

In many cases, the problem behaviors in shelter dogs come from a truly good place, but one that unfortunately, never works...the volunteers simply love too much. Not to say that love is a bad thing, but when we force our human emotions onto the world of other animals (in this case dogs), sometimes we get unintended consequences. We want to care for, touch and console a dog that has had a rough life or comes from a bad situation; but dogs, unfortunately, read the love as our approval for the unwanted behavior. By concentrating on the plight and condition of the shelter dogs rather than paying attention to the dog itself (their behavior/body language) we sometimes reward the dog for the exact problem behaviors we are looking to stop. As hard as it sounds, being able to put our human emotions aside and thinking like a dog is what it will take for these dogs to get adopted and find their forever homes. Simply put, volunteers must teach, coach and reward only those behaviors they want, and that means the behaviors prospective adopters want, not what WE think is best for the dog.

This book will focus on and introduce many of the common mistakes volunteers make with dogs, while at the same time showing how to use positive reinforcement techniques to get the behaviors that will find shelter dogs their forever homes. It will also provide specific examples on the "how to's" for redirecting dogs to choose appropriate behaviors. We are going to go from being "love blind" to a laser-like focus on the dog's problem behaviors, what causes them, and how we can correct them. This has a huge impact on getting these dogs ready for the next stage of their lives...reintroduction as pets in someone's home! We will send them on to the next chapter of their lives, only this time prepared to succeed rather than fail! So let's start with the mistakes we make or as I like to call them the "LOVE BLIND" mistakes!

So how do volunteers choose to start down the wrong path? Honestly it's very easy... They forget the first rule of training dogs...DOGS ONLY DO WHAT IS REWARDING! Put simply, if a dog has a particular unwanted behavior, then either something in the environment or something WE are doing is reinforcing that behavior. Trust me - if the behavior wasn't rewarding, no self-respecting dog would waste time doing it! Folks, now it's time to "THINK LIKE A DOG". No matter how hard we try, dogs will never be able to think like humans, and this fact alone is the reason why all of us dog trainers have jobs (thank you by the way!) For the dog/human relationships to flourish, WE must think like dogs, rather than expect dogs to "Speak English!" This is the main reason I tell my clients that I don't train dogs, I train owners. Think about it...the dogs already know how to do everything; they know how to bark, they know how to be quiet, they know how to sit, lay down, and they even know how to come back when called. The problem is some humans have yet to figure out how to ask for or reward these and other behaviors. Humans must put all that gray matter, opposable thumbs and emotion away when working with dogs, so we don't get caught up in their plight, condition or what we think they are feeling. In reality, if we would just simply watch behavior, body language and even our own actions, we would find the solution staring right back at us. Yep, we are causing and creating the bad behaviors. Sure the "we" might have been a previous owner or the dog's past experiences; but rest assured that in most cases, humans cause the problem behaviors we see in dogs.

Now that I have let the "cat out of the bag", the job falls on me not only to convince you, but to show you how to teach dogs how to make choices that will get them adopted! Let's take a look at some common problem behaviors you have undoubtedly seen at your local kennel or maybe even inside your own home. Then we can break down how they were taught and what we can do to fix them!

1. The dog barks uncontrollably every time a person walks into the kennel area or even when they see a person outside of the kennel area. In some cases, this might have bled off to barking when they see other dogs or even a paper cup blowing by their cage.

2. The dog jumps up on people. These dogs want to get their faces and sometimes their teeth as close to you and your face

as possible! It's no wonder prospective adopters' visits with these dogs are incredibly short.

3. The dog pulls like crazy when on a leash. This dog is not only a danger to the walker but to other people, animals and even the cars driving by.

4. The dog mouths or play bites. This is the dog that will engulf your hand when you interact with him. Some might be so rough that it actually hurts, or it could be that the dog just slobbers all over you, pulls at your clothes and has perfected the perfect canine body slam against your legs or side.

5. Some of the dogs might even have touch sensitivity. These dogs start play biting as a response to being touched in areas where they are uncomfortable being handled. These ares include their feet, mouth, tail, ears and private areas. Many dogs will "chew" on you if you attempt to touch these areas, while others might very well bite for real if the aversion to human touch is strong enough!

6. Others might fall into the hyperactive dog category. These dogs are so keyed up that it appears (rightly so) that they never sleep, cannot relax and are unable to calm down. They pace, bark, jump, mouth and seem to have boundless energy. Some folks might argue that this kind of dog has all the problem behaviors wrapped up in one uncontrollable package!

Want to learn how to fix these problems? Turn the page and let's get to a deeper understanding of these behaviors, why they happen and just how to begin fixing them.

3

PROVE IT...

OK, so you are thinking to yourself, all those behaviors exist not only in the dogs at the shelter but even a few of them might apply to your dog at home. But, there is no way that you as the volunteer, let alone as the dog's owner, could be the cause of these issues, is there? Well, I hate to break it to you; but yes, you are the cause of these problems. If there is anything I know for sure, you have to accept that there is a problem before you can get down to fixing it. So before I say anything about fixing these problem behaviors, I am going to break down just how human behavior and our choices shape the behavior Fido chooses in the end. Remember, DOGS ONLY DO WHAT IS REWARDING!!!! I know it sounds simple, but I promise by the end of this chapter it will not only make sense, but it will have you excited to read the rest of the book, just so you can figure out how to train differently. Some of you might even figure out how to use these techniques on coworkers, bosses and spouses!!!

Dogs are all about associations. If we react the wrong way to a bad behavior, we may unintentionally give the dog what he wants, leading him to associate a reward with bad behavior. If we do it right, the dog ends up learning that doing what we want, gets him what he wants and both of us are happy. Let's break this idea down a little further...dogs learn in a binary manner (fancy word for two way learning). In other words, if the experience is rewarding or positive, it is an iron clad guarantee that Fido is going to repeat said behavior. If, on the other hand the experience is not rewarding (did not work) no dog, including yours, will waste his time trying the behavior again!

So what do we take from this rule of behavior?

❉ If you give the most common reward, your attention, to any behavior wanted or unwanted, you are not only teaching Fido that it is OK but that you love his behavior.

❉ In other words, whether it is giving a treat, saying good boy, yelling at the dog to stop, or even resorting to touching the dog via violence or kindness, you are at some level giving your attention, which will drastically increase the likelihood that this behavior will be repeated.

❉ That's great if it is a behavior you like, but what in the world are you supposed to do if Fido is offering up behaviors you don't like and certainly don't want to continue?

Your only true weapon for eliminating unwanted behaviors is what you do with your attention. I know this sounds too simple to be true, but hopefully after reading the following examples of how we create certain behaviors (both bad and good) you will recognize that the choices you make have way more impact on Fido 's behavior that you ever realized. We will also look at how this information can be used in the shelter environment to make homeless dogs more appealing to those prospective adopters coming in looking for a forever friend.

Let's start with everyone's favorite, barking. Dogs can bark for any number of reasons, but the one thing we can be sure of is that Fido's barking is rewarding (at least to him) and you are making the barking fun! Now don't get me wrong, you might not think or realize that your actions or reactions are telling Fido to bark, bark and bark some more, but let's look at four different ways to deal with barking and you tell me if you have been reinforcing Fido's barking! By the way, three of the following examples reinforce bad behaviors, and only one is the correct choice that will actually stop the barking.

Ok, so the first example is what I like to refer to as the fight fire with fire technique; the dog barks and you yell at the dog. Let's get one thing straight "DOGS DON'T SPEAK ENGLISH!" They might be able to learn that the sound of the word "sit" means put my rump on the ground, but I could just as easily teach him that the word "pineapple sherbet" means the rump down behavior. In other words, when you yell at the dog, all the dog hears is you barking back at him and boy what a fun game this is! This one is also very common while working on the computer or talking on the phone. The dog is getting no attention so he barks; Mom or Dad yells shut up which the dog sees as getting attention; the dog learns that this barking thing really does work and the problem behavior is born. So, the next time you are about to yell at your dog, stop and think "Am I actually rewarding this behavior without realizing it?" Could there be a different way to deal with this situation?

Before we get to the right way to deal with this problem behavior, let's look at another incorrect scenario on how to handle a barking dog. The "I'm going to have to put 'em in their place" method or thinking that getting physical will fix the problem. The scene plays out like this; the dog barks, then barks again, the owner gets irritated and the dog keeps on barking. OK fast forward... owner blows up and smacks the dog or chases them out of the room to let the dog know that barking will not be tolerated. Stop and think about it, haven't you heard of those kids who get no attention from those closest to them, who then act out so they will at least get some sort of attention. In their mind, bad attention (physical or not) is better than no attention at all. I know that owning a dog can be frustrating and that anger can get the best of anyone, but trust me, this reaction from you will fix nothing and will likely damage the relationship you have with your dog. Look at it this way – didn't your dog just get you to stop what you were doing so that you would react to them? Even worse, you started a game of chase with your dog that might just become your dog's favorite new game. Whenever Fido wants to play a game of get Dad to chase me, all he has to do is run into the room and start barking. Congratulations... you have just been trained by your dog!

One last incorrect scenario to observe, and this one is going to sting for some folks, is the "I've had a really bad day" situation. This one usually happens on those days where your boss is a jerk, your biggest client changes his mind, or your better-half calls to rip you up one side and down the other. You walk in the front door and your dog is so excited to see you that he starts barking like a crazy man. All you can think is that the only person in the world who loves you unconditionally is your dog, and the next thing you know, you are rolling on the ground hugging and loving your best friend. (OK this example might be a little overboard, but you get what I mean!) Unintentionally, you just guaranteed the fact that Fido will bark every time you open the door!

If you don't believe me, think of it this way. Remember when there were payphones on every corner? (Yes, I am that old, just play along!) One day you were walking down the street and on a lark you checked the change slot on the phone and guess what, you found a quarter! Now what happens each and every time you walk by a pay phone, duh, you check the change slot. We, like dogs, don't try things because we know we will get the payout, rather we try behaviors for the chance of winning! And yes it just takes one time getting a payout (reward) for a dog or human to learn to repeat a behavior in the hopes of getting your attention.

Another way to look at these attention seeking behaviors is to think of a small child, a 2-4 year old. Those of us experienced in the world of parenting know of (and have probably learned the hard way about) the skill in which children of this age can push our buttons to get our attention or to get what they want. Guess what, your dog is doing the same thing, you just never put two and two together and got four. Don't shoot the messenger! Let's just hurry up and get to the one scenario that actually can stop an unwanted behavior.

It all comes down to how you handle, give or take away your attention. Remember earlier when I told you that dogs will not do anything unless it is rewarding? Well, all of the previous examples about barking, rewarded or gave the dog attention in some way! The fourth and only correct way of dealing with the barking issue, to finally make it stop, is to IGNORE THE DOG AND THE BARKING. Now this will not work immediately, but once Fido understands that this barking behavior is getting him absolutely nothing, it will change the behavior. Over a period of time the barking behavior extinguishes (psycho babble for stops) until Fido finds a new behavior to try. So in the end, the behaviors you see from your dog every day are direct responses to the reactions you give them. If, on the other hand, you focus on ignoring bad behaviors and paying attention to good behaviors, then you probably would not have bought this book and might just have what it takes to be a dog trainer!

There is a lot more to cover about barking, and that will be covered in a chapter 9. This was just an opportunity to prove to you that regardless of the problem behavior, it is driven by the attention given to it. So, if you are rewarding a problem behavior, even inadvertently or unawares, you are making it worse. And I'm sure you wonder what if these behaviors are so ingrained that this simple technique of ignoring the behavior and the dog does not seem to work? Well turn the page and wel-come to the world of REDIRECTION, the second part of ignoring the dog after the reward has been given.

4

REDIRECTION...

So at this point we recognize how we give and withdraw attention can have a huge impact on behavior. Trust me though, there are going to be times you will not be patient enough or willing to wait long enough for the behavior to go away on its own... In those cases, there is one other trick I can teach you to speed up the process. You can use redirection in how you give or take away attention from Fido. Now I don't want to get all "psychology guy" on you but... Remember that we have already determined that if a behavior is rewarding, it increases, and if it is not rewarding, it extinguishes (or goes away). What we have not talked about is the time frame an unwanted behavior has been occurring and how that directly ties to the length of time it takes to make that behavior go away. Take for example a puppy that has only been barking for attention for a month or two; it is pretty obvious that this behavior could be extinguished relatively quickly using the ignoring technique. On the other hand, if a dog has gotten away with this attention seeking barking for

4-5 years, the process is going to take quite a bit longer to extinguish.

What I suggest is a technique that will "supercharge" the idea of ignoring and make the extinguishing process happen much faster. I am going to choose another (or replacement) behavior besides barking, and reward that new behavior in the absence of the barking. This is called redirection. The key to redirection is that you, with or without a trainer's help, have to sit down and decide just what behavior you want from your dog instead of the unwanted behavior. If you do not start off with a new behavior picked out and ready before you start, you will fail. So for the problem behavior of barking, I choose to reward the behavior of looking me in the face or what I call a "Watch Me" command.

A little known secret is that dogs typically don't have the attention span to walk and chew gum at the same time; so this command is very handy for redirection. The dog is barking, so I am ignoring the dog. I then wait for a pause in noise (you know for the dog to breathe) and then ask for the watch me command. The moment I get eye contact, I reward him with a treat! This builds the relationship for the dog that barking gets me ignored, while quietly paying attention, and looking Mom/Dad in the face, gets me a tasty treat...

For arguments sake, we are going to pick another problem behavior...JUMPING UP...to illustrate how to use redirection. Don't worry, as with barking, we will cover jumping up in greater detail in Chapter 10.

We know that if we yell at the dog for jumping up, it will reward the dog and likely excite him as well, leading to repetition of the behavior. We also know that pushing or attempting to knock the dog down physically will only lead to a great game of "pogo stick" (dog comes up, you push dog down, dog comes up, etc. what a fun game!) And finally, if you have a bad day at work, then love, touch or otherwise pay attention to our dog while he is jumping up; well you are getting what you deserve!

You have tried really hard to simply ignore the jumping behavior, but you just don't have the time, patience or inclination to put up with this behavior any more...so now what? Simple, we add the idea of REDIRECTION to our efforts! The secret is the command "sit"...

The first step to this process is simple, we need to identify a behavior we want instead of the "jumping". In my mind, the only option is "Sit." Let's face it, a dog that is sitting is not jumping; and isn't that what we want? Not to mention, I teach all of my dogs that the command of "sit" is the doggy version of the human word please. If you want something, you better say please (hey, I expect the same from my kids!) If you want to go out the door, "sit." If you want to have your leash put on, "sit." How about a little dinner, fine, then you "sit." I don't care what your thoughts on dog training might be, but I believe that a dog sitting is most likely a dog being good! The next step is to make sure your pooch understands and is extremely reliable with the command "sit." To ensure you have a reliable "sit", I suggest taking the next week or so and practice "sit" every day, all day; and then practice some more. Use treats and access to desired resources (food, toys, pets, leash...you name it) and by the end of this practice Fido will be offering "sit" without you even requesting it; because in Fido's mind "my chances of getting what I want go way up when my butt is on the ground."

Now, let's get back to redirection. We still have to ignore the jumping up behavior whenever it is offered. I don't mean just kind of ignore; I mean you don't make eye contact, you don't touch, you don't talk to Fido; I mean absolutely no response. I even tell folks to walk out of the room and shut a door on the dog if necessary. If Fido jumps up, you are to give him the cold shoulder for at least 10 to 20 seconds. If you have one of the real stubborn pooches that will jump on your back or follow you while jumping, just leave the kennel or room and shut a door between you, anything you can do to physically separate you from the dog. Remember, the goal here is for the dog to lose total access to you. After all, isn't access to you exactly what the dog wants? The problem here is that the dog has learned how to push your buttons and get you so frustrated that you "blink" first and reinforce the behavior. Today we turn the tables and use a little Psych 101 on Fido by introducing a replacement behavior.

We know that dogs only do what is rewarding, right? So after a period of what psychologists call an extinction burst (we call it a temper tantrum), the dog will give up on the old tried and true behavior of jumping all over you to get your attention and try something new. If you have done as we discussed, Fido knows that "sit" almost always gets him what he wants, and if jumping isn't going to work anymore, why not try putting his butt on the ground. That behavior always seems to work! If done correctly we just made jumping not rewarding (no attention) and created a replacement behavior ("sit") that leads to the wanted reward, attention. Pretty simple concept huh? Fido jumps up and gets blown off; puts his butt on the ground and gets a treat in his mouth with some love and pets from you...which would you choose? I need to share a word of caution here... you had better be prepared to react the instant Fido's butt hits the ground! Have some treats handy (in your pocket, not in a container in the kitchen) and jackpot Fido with 2-3 treats and lavish him with love the entire time the butt is on the ground. However, if Fido breaks out of the sit and gets excited by your praise and jumps again, turn around and ignore him, starting the entire process again. Before you know it (if you are consistent) your dog will have decided on his own, that sitting works way better as a way to get your attention!

Congratulations are now in order! YOU have just allowed your dog to teach himself by choosing between two behaviors; one desirable (sitting, getting treats, attention and praise) vs. the other unpleasant (jumping up and being ignored.) Now even the slowest among us can put this equation together... butt on ground = love and treats or jump up = be ignored. Honestly which one would you choose? I am willing to bet that I know which one the dog will pick!

You have just learned one of the great truths, the $64,000 question or the Holy Grail of dog training. Got a problem behavior? First ignore it, then replace it and finally... reward the hell out of the replacement behavior. The result: no problem behaviors since dogs only do what is rewarding.

After the last two chapters you have a basic understanding of how unwanted behaviors develop as well as techniques on how to attack those nasty little buggers and get Fido headed back down the right path. The next chapter takes on dog training in a more specific manner with some basic nuts and bolts as well as the age old argument should we use punishment or reinforcement to teach our furry four legged friends.

5

HOW TO TALK LIKE A TRAINER....

I really promise to try and not kill you with the terms and definitions in this chapter. I will deal exclusively with the "how to", and only briefly cover the names us snotty professionals call these wonderful ideas! My goal is for you to feel comfortable with the ideas and principles of not only the "how to" but also the "why" things work in dog training. Keep in mind, I am a positive reinforcement dog trainer and my ideas might be new to you. Some of you might not even like my ideas, but please have an open mind. You never know, you just might find a totally new way at looking at dogs and their behavior! So let's get started...

Before any training can take place, you need to understand several ideas;

1. A way to let Fido know he did something right.
2. A way to let Fido know he did something wrong.
3. A way to let Fido know close but no cigar!

4. A way to let Fido know he is done working.

In the fancy world of Dog Training these ideas are known, respectively, as the positive mark, negative mark, no reward mark and release word. Now that you have the terms, I will focus on the ideas and simply speak to you in a common sense, nuts and bolts manner. After all, all I want is for you to understand how to apply the ideas, not pass a test on them!!!

Let's start with the positive mark, or how we tell Fido that he has gotten something right! I would suggest using a word or even a noise, but that depends on what is available to use. If you have a clicker (hand held noise maker); the sound of the clicking noise becomes your way to mark, or tell Fido great job! If you do not have a clicker, then just use a word. My favorite is the phrase "Thank You" which lets Fido know he got it right and that you are ready to reward him. Keep in mind that the reward itself is probably as important as the noise or word. The goal here is to associate a particular "wanted" behavior with a word or sound that lets the dog know all is good in the world and a reward is coming! Yes, that means that when you click or say thank you, you will follow up quickly with a reward (a tasty morsel) and before you know it you have a dog working for a paycheck (treats) by giving you the behavior you want. Timing is critical here! If you are not clicking and rewarding the instant you get the expected behavior from Fido, he may associate the reward with a behavior that you don't necessarily want.

Now, there are going to be times when Fido is just not getting it and his behavior is, well, unwanted. We must not only have a way to say "that's what I wanted" but we also need to have a way to say "Not even close, what are you thinking?" This is called the negative mark. Now, by the normal definition of mistake, you might think the negative mark is all about the dog making an error and us humans reacting to the mistake by saying something like "Bad Dog." In reality, it has very little to do with letting Fido know he has made a mistake. Instead, it is all about getting your dog's attention so you can "REPLACE" the bad behavior with something else that can be rewarded! (Remember redirection?) If you find your dog engaging in a behavior you do not like, what is the first thing you need? Well if it were me, I would want a way to get his attention so he would stop the unwanted behavior to give me a chance to ask for something I did want (replacement behavior). With all that being said, all I want you to understand is that the negative mark is way more about interrupting bad behavior than it is about disciplining or correcting it.

I use the sound "eghhh." It is hard to describe and even harder to spell, but imagine the word egg without the hard "g" sound at the end. You can even double this noise making it more like Eghhh..Eghhh. Whichever noise you choose, the goal is to get the dog's focus off the unwanted behavior and back on you, so that you can ask for and thus teach a desired replacement behavior. Keep in mind, the only goal of the negative mark is to gain attention. I say this, because the most common mistake I see with this technique is that people go overboard with both volume as well as venom in the tone of their voice. In some cases it will scare the dog and in others it will ratchet up the energy level of the dog making the bad behavior more intense. Either way, it ends up killing any chance you have to get their attention and redirect the behavior. Remember that your negative mark sound just needs to be distinctive enough to get Fido's attention without being too loud or mean so as to scare him.

You now have your positive and negative marks, but what if the behavior is just a little off. This is what trainers call the "no reward mark". Let me explain it a bit differently. What if Fido gives a behavior that is an OK behavior, but not necessarily the one you ask for? You ask for a sit and get a down or maybe even a shake? This "not quite correct" behavior is simply one you want to shape into something else. It is not a "BAD" behavior; it is just one that you have not asked for. So what is a "no reward mark"? It is a noise or word that an owner can use to let their dog know to keep trying or you almost got it, just keep trying. I simply use the word "nope "or "try again" as a way to let Fido know to keep working and to offer something else. This allows the dog the opportunity to work through the problem to figure out the correct behavior. I will also offer the command word (such as "sit" or "down") again to reinforce the behavior I am asking for. It is important to remember not to repeat the command word over and over and over in quick succession, as the dog can begin to tune you out.

As with all dog training, I am always ready with a reward so that when they finally do get the answer right, I can immediately reward it. In many areas of learning, dog or people, this idea is referred to as shaping a behavior and is actually a lot of fun. Think back to when you were a kid and you played the game hot and cold. The closer you got to the right answer, your friend would say hotter, hotter, man you are really hot. Or, if you were on the wrong track, it would be colder, colder, man you are freezing!

The last term or bit of vocabulary that every dog trainer/ owner/volunteer needs to know is a way to let Fido know that he and you are done working. This is the "release word". So far we have about every angle covered on how to let the dog know what we want or don't want, but we have yet to learn how to tell the dog we are done! If I put my dog in a really long sit-stay, is it meant to last forever? Now enter the phrase of "all done", my "release word". Some of the other release words I have heard used are; free dog, recess, go play or party time. I could care less what you say, I just want you to make sure you have a noise or word that lets your dog know he is done and can get back to his doggy stuff, rather than continuing to paying attention to you. Granted, my release word is pretty boring, but for me it indicates we're finished working and it was also easy for me to remember!

So you now know the words that many of us dog trainers use and have a pretty clear idea of when, where, how and why to use them, but there is still one HUGE issue regarding dog training that we have yet to cover, and this one is where dog trainers split into different camps. It is on whether we should or how to use reinforcement and/or punishment. Well this is an issue near and dear to my heart and one that we are going to jump into feet first in the next chapter!

Now for dog training's dirty little secret... to use punishment or not to use punishment... that is the question we cover next.

6

THE GOOD THE BAD AND THE UGLY...

OK...let's get this one out of the way right now! You cannot teach dogs without both reinforcement and punishment. Many "positive reinforcement" trainers may have just thrown this book across the room and/or burned it in their garage, but relax and keep reading. I have not lost my mind, nor gone to the dark side, but I must make a distinction here, no trainer, reward-based or correction-based, can effectively train a dog with only one side of this equation! Let me try to explain with a quick lesson in psychological history.

In 1905, Edward Thorndike proposed The Law of Effect and, in my opinion, modern day research psychology began. He drew the conclusion that all learning was binary (two-way) and that anything pleasurable would be repeated, becoming stronger, and anything unpleasant would become weaker and eventually extinguish from a behavioral standpoint. The fact is, learning is a two way street. You cannot have good without bad, white without black or reward without punishment! Let me be clear, my definition of punishment and other's definitions are probably very different! I come from a background based on a bachelor's degree in psychology, and to me, punishment simply means "anything that decreases the frequency of a behavior." Some trainers look at the word punishment as being synonymous with harshness or even pain. For me, punishment is not, shall not, and will never be cruel, painful or physically coercive. It could be a time out, withholding of attention, or the end of a fun game of tug! In the end, it must make the subject decide to change their own behavior so that they, the subject, get what they want...something rewarding. This strengthens the behavior and increases the likelihood of making the right choice, while subsequently weakening the wrong choice since that choice brings about no reward or reason to repeat.

The idea of positive reinforcement dog training burst on the scene back in the early 80's, and in many cases took off like wildfire! It was awesome, many in the industry were changing, others were rethinking their techniques and things for canines were getting better. Unfortunately, like everything else, humans have a tendency to ruin a good thing. They began to forget the dichotomy of learning and began to villainize the punishment side of learning. The pendulum swung completely the other way and trainers started saying things like "I am a 100% positive reinforcement trainer." Some even went so far as to attack trainers with different views (some did deserve this, but not all). It got so bad that most trainers became apprehensive of even using the word punishment due to the bad "juju" the word now conjured up.

Fast forward to recent history and now we have not only taken the word punishment out of training but also, in many cases, anything that resembles it. On the surface, this sounds like a great idea, but as with all utopian ideas, once you get what you think you want, only then do you realize what was left out. In this case, we've created a world of dogs that have lost much of their reliability and are totally reward motivated. In other words, we have dogs that only work when they can see a reward. And in many cases they can't focus for more than a few moments before losing concentration due to lack of impulse control! Why? For years we relied too heavily on the idea of treats and/or rewards (only positive reinforcement) creating a generation of spoiled brats, interested more in what they got, rather than the work needed to earn it! Business leaders refer to this as the WIIFM (What's in it For Me) Syndrome.

Let me see if I can put this entire idea into a metaphor for easier understanding. We'll compare a slot machine to a pop machine. In many ways today we have become pop machines in our dog's eyes. We are simply dispensers of treats and rewards. For every buck and a half that goes in, a pop comes out, right? Think about it, how do you feel when you put that buck and a half in a pop machine, push the button and no pop comes out? You better believe it; you get a little cranky, right? You might even kick or shake the machine. Now think about it from a dog's perspective. Up until this point, every time you asked Fido for something, you gave him a treat. Now out of the blue, you decide you must be the boss and require the dog to work without receiving a treat, even though you asked for a behavior that used to get Fido a reward. Well pardon my French, but in most cases the dog is now thinking to heck with you, without the treat I am not doing squat! And without intending to, you have created a treat junkie!

The other side of this proverbial coin is the slot machine! This is what we should be striving for, the idea that a dog will work for the chance to get a reward, not the reward itself. Those of you who have gambled already understand this. You don't walk up to a slot machine put in a dollar and expect to win. Instead you play the game for the chance and the hope to win or be rewarded. Each and every time one of these "random" rewards comes, the wanted behavior becomes more and more strongly ingrained! You continue to feed money into the slot machine in the hopes of another payout.

We are going to delve deeper into the idea of pop machines and slot machines in the next chapter when we continue the discussion on random and continual rewards. We will be looking at the difference between Luring and Bribing when rewarding dogs for their behaviors next.

7

LURES VS. BRIBES...

My goal with this chapter is to answer two questions:

1. Will I always have to use treats in training?
2. Just when am I supposed to use treats?

Both questions can be answered by learning the difference between lures and bribes. One road takes us to reliability, hard work and a dog that patiently waits for our next request. The other road leads to a spoiled, inattentive and distractible goon, that can't sit still for more than a couple of seconds without losing it. Ironically as I wrote the last chapter and now write this one, I have to giggle at the parallels between the topic of dog training and the state of our world today. I guess if I am lucky, maybe this book will be able to transcend dog training!!! Ok, sorry, back to the dogs.

Luring always has and always should have a place in teaching anything. Let's use the example of teaching a dog to sit as a way to greet people (this one is huge from a stand point of shelter dogs anyway). The first step we take is to show or lure the dog how to sit, right? Start by taking a treat and letting the dog smell and get interested in it. Then, move the treat up and over the dog's head very slowly. As the dog tries to follow the treat, physics take control, where the nose goes the butt will soon follow and bang, the rear end touches the ground. The dog has completed his first successful "sit" on command! As I repeat this process, I begin to either make noise with a clicker or say the words "thank you" as a way to mark the behavior of the rear end touching the ground. In other words, every time the rump hits the ground the behavior is marked and a treat is given. As I reach 6- 12 successful repetitions, the dog makes the connection that the hand movement or cue of flipping my hand above or near his head equals his rear end touching the ground and that he gets a treat! Now we come to the crossroad...do we keep luring the behavior by paying for the behavior before it happens or do we place the expectation on the behavior that you "sit" first and the reward comes later? This my friends is where all the problems in dog training come from. We have become so fix-ated on the positive side (the treat) of training that we forget to fade the lure (which becomes the reward) and are now bribing Fido to give a behavior.

Ask yourself a simple question "does your boss pay you before or after you do the work"? After - right? This is where we have to delve into a little psychobabble, but it is necessary to drive the point home. The way you reward a behavior is called a reward schedule, and there are tons of variations and versions, but for this example we are going to focus on just two versions: let's call them continual and random reward schedules. Con-tinual means giving a reward or treat every time a behavior is presented and random means giving the reward at varying times so the dog or subject never really knows when the reward is coming. In our earlier example of "sit" we can suffice it to say that if you continue giving treats every time Fido puts his rump on the ground it is a continual reward and you are becoming a pop machine. But if you are mixing it up, keeping the dog guessing, you are randomly rewarding him and evolving into a slot machine. You are taking the first steps to getting your pooch to work for the chance of a reward! Hopefully the light bulb is starting to flicker!!! If not, no worries, just keep reading, it gets better!

Let's look at the dog whose owner keeps treating every time. As time goes on, the dog begins to expect the reward before doing the work and when you attempt to slow the use of treats or accidentally forget to have them with you... it is not a pretty site. It's similar to you not getting your pop from the machine after paying for it, the dog becomes frustrated, and the behavior falls apart. The expected payout is not coming and the dog does not understand why. Lures are critical in the actual learning of a new behavior, but if they are not faded out they only become a distraction (a bribe.) So after the magic 6 to 12 repetitions of Fido doing a behavior correctly, we have to immediately shift to rewarding on a random payout schedule so that the dog realizes that the treat doesn't always accompany the "sit" but does come often enough that I had better pay attention.

What if I told you there was yet another version of reward scheduling we could move to that would make behavior even more reliable? This one is just the next logical step in how to correctly use food or treats in dog training, and it is called a deferential reward schedule. With this technique, rewards or treats are dependent on the quality or speed of the given behavior. Put simply, I will still be rewarding on a random schedule, but will now only reward the best versions of the behavior. First, we started by rewarding or luring every time Fido got the behavior correct, which can be thought of as learning the new behavior. We then moved to randomly rewarding the correct behavior to teach the dog that work comes first and the paycheck comes second. The problem with stopping here is that by rewarding randomly you are rewarding some great behavior and some just OK behavior. Finally, if we evolve or move on to the idea of deferential rewarding, you will then only reward the best behavior. For example, if I introduce my dog to a friend and we don't get the "sit" immediately for the greeting and I have to ask for the "sit", is this really the behavior I want to reward and thus reinforce? What if the dog walks right up to the stranger and plops the rear end down and patiently waits for a pet? For me, this is the behavior I want to reinforce. So the idea of rewarding a dog becomes not only random, like a slot machine, but is now also dependent on the quality of the behavior. With that you can say you are now on the road to that rock solid reliability that we all want and a dog that patiently waits for your next request.

Now that we have a really good understanding of dog training basics, we must get back to the meat and potatoes of this book...the six most common problem behaviors we see in shelters today.

8

WELCOME TO THE PROBLEM BEHAVIORS...

Let's take a look at shelter life or home life for that matter, and see just how we affect dogs without even realizing it. When you get right down to it, many of the problem behaviors shelter dogs exhibit are the same ones that regular pet dogs have as well. These behaviors are likely the reasons so many dogs are being surrendered to begin with. Unfortunately, these problem behaviors that exist in shelter dogs start them off with 1 or 2 strikes against them right off the bat! This is before they even get a chance to arrive at their new homes! So we need to familiarize ourselves with some of the most common problem behaviors that occur in shelters. That way we can understand why they happen and what we can do to fix them. After all, a dog coming back to the shelter after only a couple of days in their home is probably one of the saddest things the shelter staff has to deal with. Here are the ones we will cover:

1. Barking
2. Jumping up or on people
3. Pulling on a Leash
4. Mouthing/Play biting
5. Touch Sensitivity
6. Hyperactivity

Before we get down to specifics, let's look at dog problem behaviors in the big picture. Why do dogs do anything, whether it's wanted or unwanted? To put it simply, it's because the behavior is rewarding. No dog, person, boss, spouse or child is going to engage in any behavior unless it gets them something in return. With that in mind, it is time to put on your doggy detective hat, step back and look at Fido's behavior and figure out just what he is getting by acting the way he is. If you do this and are honest with yourself and with the answer you come up with, you will note that in 98% of the issues, it is you or the previous owner that are rewarding the unwanted behaviors! Don't get mad! I did not say you were doing it on purpose or even realized it was happening, but as you are about to learn, even though largely unintentional, it is people that create the majority of issues we see in dogs today.

Just how are we doing this, you ask? It could be incidental eye contact, a word (either happy or angry), a touch (out of frustration or out of love), heck it could be any reaction you give while the unwanted behavior is taking place. You don't have to see it as a reward. If Fido thinks it is rewarding, a behavior is born.

Think about it, you are on the computer or phone and Fido starts barking, and you give him a dirty look...yep you reinforced the barking. Your dog is jumping all over you and you push him away and yell "no"...yep you reinforced the jumping.

How about when your dog is being all crazy and you chase him all over the house telling him to stop...yep you reinforced the hyperactivity! Now look at these examples again and ask yourself "What is Fido getting out of this scenario that is reinforcing the behaviors?" Bingo! Fido is getting your attention. Congratulations Ladies and Gentlemen, you just found the secret weapon to making dog training work! What is the one thing on earth your dog wants more than anything (treats included)? Yep, it's your attention!

Going forward, I am going to explain specific problem behaviors and show how, by giving or withholding attention, how you can make a behavior stronger (the ones you want) or weaker to the point of eventually stopping (the ones you don't want). It really is just that easy. The hard part is whether you have the patience and consistency to suppress your reactions towards Fido long enough to get what you want. After all, aren't we the species with the opposable thumbs and all that grey brain matter we like to brag about?

The next few chapters will focus on these common problem behaviors in detail, so read on!

9

BARKING...

This behavior is near and dear to me as a dog trainer, and I am going to start off by making some folks mad. Dogs are social animals and belong inside a home, not outside one. So, if you are one of those folks who has a dog that never comes inside (barring those folks where Fido has a specific job like on a farm), or whose neighbors are complaining, or you have a court date next Thursday, and you call a trainer saying you refuse to let your dog inside but still want them to quit barking, I CAN NOT HELP YOU until you decide to help yourself! It is not any better in the shelter world, which never seems to have enough space or foster parents to go around. They are forced to put dogs outside, alone, for extended periods of time. In either case, the only solution to stop the barking is to understand why it is happening and just what can be done to improve the situation.

So what makes barking one of the hardest problem behaviors to fix? Actually, it is because barking is a combination of boredom and the fact that the act of barking actually feels good!

Some scientists even suggest that the act of barking releases endorphins or "feel good drugs" in the dog's brain! This tells us right off the bat the behavior itself is rewarding. And to complicate things, in most cases you are not even present when the barking is happening. Let's face it, if you are in the house (or at work) and the dog is outside in the yard barking, how are you going to correct or even attempt to reward an alternative behavior?

I know all of this makes it sound like the problem is unsolvable (and it is a tough one), but what if we look at it from a different point of view? Why don't we address the behavior from the prevention side? Let's eliminate the barking before it gets started, and before all that self-rewarding stuff happens...

For that to work, we need to start with a little doggy detective work into the "why" dogs bark. I will focus on the three main causes: boredom, anxiety and reaction to things the dog experiences. Trust me there are others, but in my mind if we deal with these three main causes, most barking and even some other "bad" behaviors are likely to go away. And these are some of the main issues seen in kennels and shelters.

Boredom is a huge problem with dogs today. We live in a world where everyone is working or busy. Leash laws and litigation have taken away many natural ways for dogs to socialize. There is also the misconception that the backyard gives Fido plenty of exercise. Think about it...the dog is left alone with nothing to do but bark, chew, pee, poop, and sleep (you know...normal dog stuff) because no one has ever taught him to do anything else when bored. Just what did you expect the dog to do? Dogs must be allowed to use their minds to deal with boredom just like we do.

Humans, for the most part, can find constructive ways to deal with boredom, but for some reason we expect our dogs to deal with their boredom, not like a dog, but constructively, like a human. Add to that, we typically do not give our dogs instruction as to what we want. This happens in the shelter world as well. There is not enough staff, the volunteers have little training, and if lucky, the dogs get a thirty minute walk every other day.

Let's look at barking from the point of view of the shelter:

✳ Dogs are rarely allowed to be together and play. In many cases, it is because they are dog aggressive and putting them together would result in a fight. But in every shelter I have ever been to, I have never seen one where all of the dogs are "reactive". The solution is to create "stop light" categories: red dogs, yellow dogs and green dogs! This idea will also be critical in the training of volunteers, but for now let's just say we are going to start by categorizing dogs by energy level and social ability. In other words, green dogs get to play with green dogs, yellow dogs play with yellow dogs and red dogs will not interact socially with other dogs. This program will take time to institute, but the dogs and the volunteers deserve it. You will have to dedicate a staff member who knows dog behavior to run the play yard and to decide who plays with who and for how long. You will need to understand that the green dogs are typically the wild and crazy pups who like to give and receive body slams and run like crazy. The yellow dogs are the older/elder statesmen who still like to interact, but not at such a high rate of speed. The red dogs however, are the dogs that just don't appreciate play with other dogs for any number of reasons and will end up playing by themselves or with the volunteers if deemed appropriate.

✻ Worried you won't be able to find a suitable person? I'll bet there is a local dog trainer looking to supplement their income or who has dreams of making a difference in the shelter world that would fit this bill nicely! Once this idea is up and running, how many more dogs will be adopted? Especially now that in addition to having burned off some energy, they have been given the bonus of social interaction with other dogs? Remember, we should be rewarding or encouraging the behaviors potential adopters want, not what is easiest for the shelter.

✻ What about a play yard with agility equipment? Did you know you can make almost all of your own equipment out of PVC pipe for very little money? And the plans are right there on the internet! If you think outside the box, I bet you could get a Boy Scout Troop looking for Eagle Projects to do the work for you; and once done you have a great way to relieve boredom for both dogs and volunteers! It may even be a way to make some money for the shelter doing "Fungility Classes" for other dogs on the weekends! Plus, this is a great way for red dogs to get some exercise and work their brains while they work with the volunteers.

✳ Buy a set of Rally Obedience cards and have a Rally class every quarter for volunteers (again if you have a trainer that can teach this, it is a great money maker for the shelter!) Spend the time to teach the volunteers how the sport works, and have them take a dog through the class. After they have been through just one class, how many other dogs could that volunteer positively affect! For those who don't know what Rally is, it is an obedience course where dogs go from station to station doing basic commands! Again, it would not take much to build a custom course for the dogs and volunteers to use. Trust me, the brain power used here is way more than just sitting in a cage or even going on a walk. As you are probably figuring out, I do believe every shelter should have a certified trainer on staff who is employed by the shelter.

✳ Feed your dogs from toys. To heck with the food bowl...let Fido burn some energy and time trying to figure out how to get frozen food out of a Kong; or dog food with peanut butter out of a Squirrel Dude or better yet; what about a Buster Cube that they have to knock around to get the food out? Instead of wasting 60 seconds on a meal out of a bowl, make lunch time last 10 to 15 minutes and let the dog actually get something out of dinner time!

Yeah, I can hear it now, I don't have the time, I don't have the staff, yet you tell everyone who will listen to you that your goal is to get every last dog adopted with as few returns to the shelter as possible! Let me clue you into a little secret: DOING THE SAME THING OVER AND OVER AND EXPECTING DIF-

FERENT RESULTS IS THE DEFINITION OF CRAZY! Not to mention the goal of this book is to train volunteers. I bet once these ideas have been introduced, the volunteers would be more than happy to fill Kongs or other food puzzles!

So let's discuss the idea that time alone in a yard without some sort of enrichment (fancy word for something to do) can be called exercise. Trust me, once the dog has smelled, seen, felt, touched and tasted everything in the "yard" (it will take maybe three visits) it's a pretty damn boring place to spend their day. They have known this for years in the zoo world, so why has it taken so long to get the word out in the shelter world? Trust me, all it is going to take is a paper cup blowing by the fence and the barking begins again. Need a human metaphor as an example?

Think back to your first job. Whether you had a cubicle, classroom, office or some other type of space, your first day was so cool, putting up family pictures, a desk calendar or maybe even hanging your diploma up on the wall. That space was the most stimulating environment you had ever experienced; you were productive, happy to have your own little place in the world. Now fast forward 6 months and you will do almost anything in your power to get out of that space because it is now boring as hell! That initial excitement and shine of your new workspace has been worn away, and you now look for any diversion or distraction you can find to break up the monotony. So, why are we shocked when the same thing happens to dogs?

I know I have already covered this, but let me say it again. If you plan to incorporate a doggy day care or play yard, you will have to monitor and manage the process. You will need to have someone with knowledge of dogs and dog behavior. You don't want to see what happens when you just throw 6 Kongs into a pen full of dogs. Take the time to do it right and get the right people on your team. The result will be dogs who are no longer bored with life or barking 24-7. Instead, you now have dogs that spend more time napping because their heads and bodies are tired! (Hint, hint...I am again saying you need an on staff trainer!)

Anxiety barking is another problem that even though somewhat different, is in many ways treated with the same ideas. If a person, or dog for that matter, is anxious, that anxiety will definitely affect both personality and behavior; but if kept busy with a project or activity, many times the barking begins to lose intensity and frequency. Many of the ideas we have already covered are great places to start when the dogs are showing anxiety, fear or nervousness as their reason for barking. But how do you know what these behaviors are or even what they look like? I think the best description of them is the inability to focus, primarily due to everything else going on in the world. It's kind of like being hyper-sensitive or scared of the world. These dogs might bark at other animals, people, or even inanimate objects that startle or surprise them. This might not be the most accurate description of anxiety but let's face it, we need to be able to imagine what this type of dog looks like, not define it.

In most cases, anxiety in dogs is created one of two ways.

· First, there was an event or time period that has fractured the dog's way of looking at the world. Instead of a normal looking world, their world is full of the unexpected and the unknown, which to a dog like this equals fear. Sometimes it can be a bad experience in the middle of the dog's life or it might be isolation during the critical socialization period of puppyhood.

.   Second, the instance when the dogs are hardwired wrong. Put simply, the dogs have problems born from issues of neurology, biology and/or genetics. The only thing in common to these causes, is a dog that is afraid, over-stimulated and/or not capable of dealing with the world in a way we would consider normal.

The aspect we have to get past is the "why" the barking is happening. There is no way for a dog to talk to us or tell us what or how they are feeling. We are left to simply observe the unwanted behaviors and work to replace them with more rewarding good behaviors. A very wise man once told me "you can always change behavior, but you will never change personality".

The exception to this would be those wiring issues mentioned before; sometimes a veterinarian can improve the situation with medication. This is why I always recommend a trip to the vet before calling in a trainer. It is best to rule out medical issues before trying to train away or improve a behavior. Medical reasons notwithstanding, to improve this type of barking will require a combination of exercise to wear out the mind, while also using counter conditioning and operant conditioning. What this means is that by using repetition, you take what is scary or over stimulating and make it more rewarding and/or normal, through the use of positive reinforcement rewards based training.

You, as a volunteer, or as an individual dog owner can do a lot to improve dog behavior, but if I am describing a dog you have or know of in the shelter, please get a professional involved immediately to help you. Pushing a dog too hard or too fast can lead to disastrous results. There are only three things you (or

Fido) can do when anxious, Freeze, Flight and finally Fight. A professional trainer will be able to help you read the dog in question and determine their body language and know when to pull back and not push too hard. This will keep everyone, including you and the dog, safe. We will cover this aspect of dog behavior in much more detail coming up in the section about dog body language and staying safe.

The last topic I will discuss is how to deal with reactionary barking. As you get deeper into problem barking, you can see all of the forms of barking are really not separate issues but really a three headed monster all wrapped up together. Reactionary barking also has to do with over-stimulation. This could manifest itself in many ways such as:

❋ Fido is able to see other dogs and Fido begins barking because he wants to play (Frustration)

❋ Fido doesn't like other dogs, so he barks to make the other dogs go away (Territorial)

❋ Fido is so bored that if anything catches his attention, he barks (Nothing to do)

❋ Barking could even be a predatory issue where Fido sees a squirrel, something small, fuzzy and movin fast, so he barks (and if given the chance, chases)

All of these causes share one thing in common; the barking is in reaction to something else. In most cases, fixing or working on reactionary barking becomes a management issue rather than a training issue. What I mean by that is, it is way easier to eliminate the things creating the barking than try to teach a dog that barking is bad! Let's face it... barking is one of those things that makes a dog a dog! Even if you don't like hearing this, you know it is true! So how do we fix it?

One solution specific to a shelter environment is to build blinds between outdoor kennels or use shower curtains between the cages inside the shelter. This is so dogs cannot see the other dogs in the cages right in front or to the side of them. This idea even works in the home as well. Does your dog bark while sitting in front of the huge picture window at the front of the house? Have you tried shutting the blinds, installing drapes or using roman blinds (the fancy ones that are only at the bottom of the window)? An easy way to try the "Roman Blind" idea is by taping wax paper to the window at the bottom of the window or spraying aerosol Christmas Tree Flocking on the window (it can be scraped off with a razor blade later). The goal is to find anything that blocks Fido's view, while still allowing you to see out of the top of the window, to reduce his ability to see things outside that make him bark. I know these ideas seem really simplistic, but they do work. Is it becoming clear why I chose "Keep it Simple Stupid" Dog Training for the name of my business? Always start with the simplest solution, and in most cases the situation will improve.

This brings me to a critical aspect of this book, the need to avoid problem behaviors before they start. This is accomplished by eliminating the opportunity for dogs to try and/or learn unwanted behaviors! I would much rather prevent problem behaviors, than act surprised when they show up which leads to the need to now call a trainer to fix them. Unfortunately, people love the quick fix. And as with life, dog training is no different, you get out of it exactly what you put into it. So, instead of waiting for bad behaviors to develop and the need to deal with the frustration of fixing them, why not reward the hell out of the behavior you want and IGNORE, REPLACE OR BETTER YET, PREVENT the unwanted behaviors before they even get started. Pretty simple idea huh???

10

JUMPING UP....

Fido is jumping all over you...

Whether at home or in the shelter, this one is a true pain in the a**! Not to mention that in the shelter world this behavior is a sure fire guarantee life sentence for Fido. Who on earth wants a dog that is jumping, body slamming, and trying to get his snout on the same level as yours. Heck, as you are reading this, you might even have to admit that one of your dogs at home has this joyous behavior. No problem either way, let's get down to fixing it!

Dogs jump because they want to greet you the same way they greet another dog, face-to-face. Unfortunately you are 2-3 times as tall as Fido. Not to mention you have never taught him any other way to say hello. Don't be mad at him. In the end it is either your fault he is doing this or it is now your responsibility to teach him a better way (because his last owner failed).

Let's start by teaching Fido to "sit"! All of my training (group, private or helping shelters) starts with getting this command as rock solid as possible, because it is with this simple command that I begin to teach a dog the basic idea of to how to say please! In my world and now yours, you must make Fido understand that his requirement to sit is the same as us saying please. After all, shouldn't our dogs learn to ask permission before getting something? Welcome to what I call the "sit say please" protocol...dogs must always say please before getting anything. And saying hello or greeting a person is just one example of this protocol. If Fido wants to say hello, the only way it is allowed is if his butt is on the ground and all four feet are on the floor, PERIOD...NO EXCEPTIONS!!!

In a kennel environment, teaching this is way easier than it sounds.

✳ First, you MUST get 100% of your volunteers on board with the idea of "sit say please". To start, they must get every dog to sit before they are let out of the kennel, even if for just a split second. This will take some training but what else are you going to do when you are volunteering? (more on that in Chapters 15-18)

✳ Second, start getting the dogs to offer a sit whenever you walk by their kennel. This takes nothing more than a pocket full of dog food or hanging a treat bucket at every kennel and simply walking through the kennel area. Reward those who sit when you walk up and just give some kind words to those who don't. The key is making sure the food reward only comes to the dogs that sit when you walk up. Believe me; it won't take as long as you think to get most, if not all of the dogs on board with this "non-negotiable rule". Stop and think... if all the dogs in your shelter sat when a person walked up to their kennel, how much easier would it be to get them adopted?

❊ Third, all the dogs in the kennel should be trained to sit for everything…food, going in and out of doorways, entering and leaving their kennels and especially when someone walks up to their kennel.

Remember, you are teaching the life skills these dogs need once they leave the shelter, right? You don't want to be responsible for a dog coming back because you chose not to take the time to help with their on the job training program, do you?

Now if you have this problem at home, the solution is much the same. First, you teach a super reliable "sit" so that Fido knows how to say please. Then you teach him when to say it! Here is the bad news, if your practice is not CONSISTENT, this problem is not going to go away! Fido must learn that to say hello, his butt has to be on the ground. That means if he jumps up on you, you must walk away or leave the room; even if you have to walk into a closet or the bathroom and shut the door (not kidding). Remember, all your dog really wants is your attention. It is now up to you to make him understand that if he jumps, he loses that access. If you just once forget, or allow him to jump up and get attention, good, bad or otherwise it will be you reinforcing his bad behaviors.

So you are not sure that just one mistake or instance will create a lifetime behavior in a dog??? How many of you are old enough to remember pay phones? If you are, you at some point will have found a quarter in the change slot on a pay phone. Now ask yourself a question, what did you do every time you passed a pay phone from that point on…yep, that's right, you checked the change slot for a quarter. Now remember, we are the smarter species right? So, if we can be trained to repeat a behavior after just one successful trial, why on earth would we find it so hard to believe that Fido is going to form a habit (good or bad) after just one successful or rewarding experience.

Once you have Fido realizing that jumping is no longer an option with you, you must now teach him that this "sit say please" idea must be followed with guests as well, and that means even more practice. I hate to be the bearer of bad news, but there are hundreds of other books, DVD videos and god knows what else out there that claim to have the secret cure all for all sorts of dog problems, but I am here to tell you they are all a bunch of hooey! Without practice, nothing is going to get better, and in most cases will probably get worse. Just because Fido now knows not to jump up on you, don't expect this knowledge and behavior to translate to other people.

The next step requires you to get your shoes, leash and car keys and head to the nearest pet supply store. There you have not only a captive audience of strangers; you also have an audience that likes dogs! In other words, you now have people to help you practice, and in most cases they are going to ask you if they can pet your dog. You need to get at least 50 people per week to greet your dog over the next month or two, giving Fido the chance to learn that his butt must be on the ground to say hello, which then of course leads to him getting his treat!

The how-to here is simple: first ask the stranger if they are willing to help you teach your dog how to say hello the right way. Assuming they say yes, which happens most of the time (but always ask to make sure) you, not the stranger, must ask Fido for the sit, since you are the one setting the rules. Finally, when Fido's butt is on the ground, the stranger pays for the behavior with a treat that you provide. Do this for the 30 to 60 days we have talked about, and you will have a polite dog that knows how to say hello the right way!

A final thought on this: what if someone walks up to you and asks (or in some case does not ask) to pet your dog? These are the situations where the jumping might again rear its ugly head. You must be an advocate for your dog! Do not feel bad telling someone "Excuse me, my dog can only say hello if he is sitting, so please step back and let me get him ready for you to say hello." If you don't, you are not being fair to the general public, let alone to your dog, and you and the stranger are teaching that saying hello the wrong way is OK...

Obviously you are not going to take shelter dogs to the pet store, but the same thing can be achieved by having all volunteers participate in this process and practice greets with all people in the shelter when on leash. Remember, a dog without the opportunity for real work and practice is just another dog destined for a life sentence in the shelter (or worse). So get out there and work, not only with the dogs but also with all the volunteers, to give the dogs an opportunity to learn what it takes to find their forever home.

11

PULLING ON THE LEASH...

This one happens everywhere... at the shelter, at home, out on a walk, you name it! Many dogs have no idea what this thing is that we humans keep attaching to them or even what it's for. The end result for us is a society of dogs who pull like demons and have little, if any, focus on anything while they are on leash. Let's look at a walk from the stand point of the reward for the dog. Ask yourself one simple question, "What is the reward of a walk for your dog"? Don't answer too fast, but don't think too much either; the answer is staring you right back in the face. The reward is the walk itself! So, from the "ignore the bad & reward the good" idea, if your dog is pulling or being inappropriate on a walk, what is it we must end? You bet, the walk! Now this is not a quick or easy fix of the pulling problem, but you have to understand that any behavior you don't want cannot be rewarded. It cannot be a behavior that we inadvertently reinforce. By stopping the walk every time the dog pulls, they learn that pulling is no longer a successful behavior. Up until now, the dog figures the fastest way to get from point A to point B is to drag you along for the ride. The dog (with you in tow) still gets what they want and still ends up where they want. If you were the dog, would you stop? If pulling on the leash works, it is going to just keep happening!

Now, we can do a couple of things to make the process of fixing the pulling faster and easier to deal with…

1.   Introduce an alternative behavior to compete with pulling, and once the alternative is more rewarding, the pulling will stop. In essence, you are creating a choice for the dog (replacement behavior).

2.   Use specific tools to allow the dog to choose not to pull. These come in the form of different leashes that diminish pulling while allowing you to practice walking and giving you and your shoulder a rest. There are tools I like and some I really dislike. Suffice it to say, I will only use tools that let the dog learn on their own, rather than ones that require me having to punish the dog to create the correct choice.

Let's look at how to add an alternative behavior and decide exactly what behaviors we are going to use. First, I want you to understand that when a dog is not paying attention to the owner or handler, don't be shocked if they are pulling. The goal here is to make paying attention more rewarding than just downright pulling. Remember, a dog that is paying attention and focusing on their owner is not pulling! So let's get to it, we need first to teach two commands, one you already know - "sit" and the other one is "watch me"! "Watch me" is simply the dog looking into the eyes or face of the handler on command.

Let's start with how to teach "watch me" then we'll get into how to use the command in regards to pulling. I start with a treat in my hand. I then let the dog sniff the treat. Then I move my hand to my face and point at my nose with my index finger. At the exact moment the dogs eyes meet mine, I mark the behavior with a clicker or with the words thank you and reward the dog with a treat. Once the dog has the idea, I quit luring the dog with the treat by keeping the treat behind my back in one hand and pointing at my nose with the other. That way, the dog is very quickly moving from a lure to a reward and giving me the behavior before I give the reward. Within a week, you will have a dog working great with the hand signal. This would be the point to add the words "watch me" before pointing to your nose to make sure the dog will respond with verbal and hand signals. Now for the magic, a game I call "Don't turn your back on me"!

Ok this is really easy, now that you have "watch me" down I want you to ask for a "watch me" and once the dog is looking at you, treat them and then turn your back on the dog and wait! Be patient - you might have to wait a little, but before you know it the dog will come around and look at you, now reward and be happy...your dog is now on the way to learning to walk nicely on leash. (At this point I really don't care if the dog is on or off leash, that is up to you.) Now turn around again, and again and again making sure to reward the automatic "watch me" your dog is giving you.

After several days we are going to reintroduce the idea of "sit" as well. We will do this by withholding the treat when the dog looks at you, causing the dog to wonder why this usually successful way of getting a reward is no longer working. If you have done as instructed and made "sit" equal "say please" then it will only take a couple of seconds and your dog is going to put their rump on the ground and look at you. They will offer the "sit" because it has proved to be a behavior that is usually rewarded. In other words when simply offering the "watch me" doesn't work, the dog will look back to his memory (or mental flash drive) and go with another behavior that gets a reward. BAM, reward and praise, (remember that timing is important!) now continue to work with turning your back and expecting not only a look but a "sit" each time. Get ready, here comes the next step.

Now, we add steps to the turn your back idea. Instead of just turning your back, we take a giant step in any direction and stop. Before you know it, the dog follows and comes around, looks at you and sits. What do you do now? Yep, praise and reward. Now, take a giant step in another direction and stop, then 2 steps then 3 and so on. Next thing you know you can take 5 or 6 steps and your dog is not only paying attention to you, but every time you stop your dog comes around front and sits, patiently waiting for your next command! This is the point where it becomes important to start practicing with a leash on the dog and now we enter the ideas of generalization and distractions. After all, you don't plan on walking your dog in the living room forever do you?

Keep in mind that dogs have absolutely no idea how to generalize an idea or skill from one environment to another. Not to mention if you expect your dog to have a skill (not pulling on a leash) in a distracting environment you had better be prepared to practice under distractions. If not, no amount of money spent on trainers or time spent yelling, asking or begging will improve your dog's performance. So grab your leash and head for the next step - the driveway not the sidewalk!

We have to get Fido to understand that this new walking version of don't turn your back on me is expected not only in the living room but also out in the big ole distracting world. We will also have to begin practicing in more distracting environments, but not too much too soon. We are going to start the entire process over with just "watch me", then turning your back and finally adding steps one at a time, but this time we are going to work in the drive way. Of course for safety we will use a leash, especially since we want this to translate to leash work anyway. Once we have the driveway down, we are going to take the exercise on the road! At first we are going to pick the distance from one driveway to the next, but we are going to stop and get a "watch me" and a "sit" three times in that distance, then two of each and then one. Finally, we are able to walk from one driveway to the next with no pull and with an auto sit and a "watch me" every time we stop. We then go two driveways, three driveways and so on. As we practice, we build the skill and expectation of paying attention rather than pulling, while we reinforce with Fido to actively sit at every stop and await the next direction.

So what have we learned? From the dog's perspective... first, if I pull my walk stops, second, that if I sit and look at my handler when we stop I get rewarded, and third, that staying focused on my handler rather than the distractions around me, my chances of a reward go way up. A warning: this process can be very tedious and requires a lot of patience and practice, but once taught, it will go beyond rewarding and it will open new avenues of bonding between you and your pooch! What do you do if your pulling situation is so severe that no amount of work can get the dog's attention to even get training started? Well, the first thing is to realize either you have created this situation or you are now the one who has to deal with it. This also requires you to pay attention to Fido while on the walk…you cannot just "check out" with your iPod or talk on your cell phone. Beyond that, we are going to have to utilize some external tools to get the situation and the dog under control so that you can not only burn some energy off the dog but begin the training process.

What I am talking about here are training leashes, head halters and no pull harnesses. These are tools that allow the dog to make the decision not to pull. They give you a chance to get back to ground zero as a place to start training. A word of caution, some might try to tell you that choke, prong and shock collars fit into this category and I want to make it clear they don't and explain why they have no place in my methods for training dogs. Simply put, a choke, prong or shock collar requires me to administer the correction or punishment to the dog so that Fido chooses not to pull because I have made it unpleasant. The other thing to keep in mind when you are using choke, prong or shock collars, is that you are not going to be able to effectively correct the pulling behavior unless the leash is loose. So, if the leash is loose, it means the dog is not pulling. If you correct the dog at that time, using this type of collar, you have just told the dog that the loose leash is not what you are looking for, thus the dog will be more apt to pull. It is a simple fact that whether dog, child, spouse or employee will, over time, learn to avoid individuals who deliver punishment or corrections. Rather I would want to use tools that give the dog the choice to pull or not pull based on their own actions and decisions. The head halter, no pull harnesses and specialized leashes are designed to create pressure while the dog pulls. You do not and are never to pull, tug or leash correct with these tools. You simply, as described earlier, "just stop". The dog then decides to stop pulling due to the pressure they have created by pulling. So they back up and quit pulling of their own accord and on top of all this their own behavior is self-rewarding... by not pulling the walk continues!

A final word on these tools, they are a great way to jump start training, but if they are not phased out as quickly as they are started, it will only create a crutch. They are not intended to be used for the rest of the dog's life, rather only to get you started so that the training mentioned earlier can be productive and underway quickly. I have seen way too many dogs whose owners have never faded out the use of these tools and the dog knows that if they are wearing the device it means no pulling, but if they are not wearing the device they again pull like a demon. In those cases, I believe the tools have become pun-ishing devices or at least nagging devices and the dogs have really learned nothing. Like everything in dog training, there is never a silver bullet or magic pill, only hard work and consis-tency.

My question to you is, which path will you take?

12

MOUTHING & PLAY BITING

First of all I want to be clear; there is a big difference between mouthing/play biting and real biting! If you have a dog that is drawing blood or leaving bruises all over your arms, stop reading this book and get a hold of the shelter manager or call a professional trainer and get help. However, if you simply have a dog that is mouthy, a little out of control or is just playing too rough...well then keep reading, since that is the dog we are going to talk about in this chapter, as well as ways to correct this behavior.

The first thing to understand is that the dog is not trying to hurt you; he is only trying to play and interact with you. Unfortunately, he does not realize that playing with a human and playing with another dog are two totally different things. This really makes sense when you think about it. A dog in a shelter gets minimal or no contact with people, but gets excessive contact or proximity with other dogs. So, that dog is used to interacting and playing with other dogs, but not so much with humans.

It is our job as dog owners and shelter volunteers to help dogs understand there are two sets of rules concerning play; one set when playing with other dogs and the other when playing with people. So how do you help dogs learn how to interact with other dogs? You start by simply allowing dogs to be together, under supervision. If you start small and go slowly, dogs will begin to relearn not only body language of other dogs (their way of talking) but also the appropriate level of play. This is a technique that works great, but it will take a trained eye. I do not recommend beginners (shelter or individual) to attempt dog to dog introductions or dog play groups without a trainer or experienced kennel staffer present. If you do not know how to introduce or allow play between dogs, the results could be the exact opposite of what you are looking for. It can also be downright dangerous to you and the dogs!

As we look at dogs interacting with people, we will have to do the re-training of our furry friends, and it begins with how we feed the dogs! Ok...I can just see the shocked looks from many of you now, wondering just how feeding dogs will have an effect on play biting or mouthing. Trust me it will...especially if you hand feed the dog. Yep, you heard me right! I want you to take the next 30 days and hand feed the dog only. Every piece of kibble that goes in the dog's mouth needs to come from a human hand (and the more hands the better)!

There are a couple of reasons for this technique, but mainly it stems from the saying "Don't bite the hand that feeds". As I mentioned earlier in the book, I do not agree with or use alpha theory when training dogs. I like to consider the idea that if I control all of the important things in a dog's life, then the dog understands that he/she needs me to get what they need, thus I become a leader to the dog. It requires no force, no domination and no malice to train a dog; just some simple rules like "Gentle" and "Wait" while you are hand feeding. That is what we cover next.

"Gentle" is nothing more that teaching a dog (shelter or yours at home) to take food from your hand nicely. The best comparison is that of feeding a horse. For those of you who have been around horses you understand that to feed a horse safely they eat out of the palm of your hand. You do not grasp the "carrot" with your index finger and thumb and let the horse bite your finger, right? Same thing goes for dogs. Don't make it easy for the dog to make a mistake and accidently nip a hand or finger. Rather, hide the treat behind your fingers, using your thumb to hold the food tight. The dog can sniff, lick or even chew on the front of your fingers but cannot access the food until you let the food drop into the palm of your hand and offer it to the dog! That is the technique, but we still need to introduce the word "Gentle". As the dog is sniffing, licking or chewing your hand in an attempt to get at the food, simply say the word "Gentle", and pull your hand away from the dog. Volume and venom are not necessary and can likely make the situation worse. Your tone and demeanor needs to be calm and determined, letting the dog know that the behavior is inappropriate, and until it changes, access to your hand and the food will not happen.

Think back to your own past when you screwed up somehow, and it was now time to face the music. Don't be the parent that yelled and screamed…after all we just learned to tune them out. Instead, channel the parent that would disapprovingly look at you and in the calmest voice possible say "I expected more from you and am extremely disappointed". While this technique made you feel terrible and changed your behavior, in most cases it did not make you want to avoid or hide things from your parent. By switching to this style you will immediately become a better dog trainer, spouse, parent and even person! Back to "Gentle"...once the dog relaxes and moves away from your hand, allow your hand to come back towards the dog and the treat to fall into the palm of your hand for the dog. In reality this technique is way more about impulse control than taking food but the end result is still the same, a dog who takes food nicely from a hand!

Once we have "Gentle" working and heading in the right direction, we expand the idea with a new command "Wait". This command simply takes the "Gentle" command to the next logical step. Not only do we want the dog to gently take food from us, but we also want the dog to learn to be patient. More specifically we want the dog to learn the command "Wait". We are going to teach the dog that they must back up and be patient until they are invited to take the food. Again, impulse control is our goal! The technique is pretty much the same as "Gentle", except for adding the word "Wait" and pulling the food out of the dog's reach until the dog relaxes and quits attempting to get to the food. Then you say "Gentle" and allow the dog to take the food from your hand. Trust me, both of these ideas seem pretty simple and they are. But they do not work overnight and you will have to invest weeks, if not months, in making both reliable. In fact, these are techniques that MUST be used throughout the life of a shelter dog or your dog for that matter! That should not come as a surprise if you think about "Gentle" and "Wait" as good manners rather than as commands! After all, we don't teach our kids to say please and thank you as toddlers and then forget about those sayings in grade school do we?

While these commands are great, you just might need one more word in your training arsenal to help when it comes to playing too rough. What if your dog plays with his mouth and teeth? We don't want to teach the dog not to play, but rather to learn to play in a gentler way, right? This is where we start talking about the word "Ouch". We already have the dog waiting patiently for food and taking it nicely from our hand, but "Ouch" gives us a way to deal with Fido when he makes mistakes while playing... and trust me mistakes will be made! There will be those times when play gets out of hand, or when the dog is just too excited, and the dog will inevitably nip your hand, finger, arm or any other body part. We must have a way to let the dog know a mistake has occurred, that the behavior is unacceptable and that it will not be tolerated (without us being a total jerk in the process!) The answer is the word "OUCH"... now let's learn how.

Once again, this word has no need for volume or venom. Any time (and I mean any time, even if it did not hurt) the dog's teeth touch your skin; I want you to say Ouch! Pull your hand away, get up and ignore the dog for about 15 seconds (no longer than 30 seconds). The tone of the OUCH should be one of pain and sorrow (to make it sound like you're in pain). We want the dog to think they actually hurt you and that you stormed off like a little brother would, if you hurt him during play. So the ouch is similar to a yelp by a dog sibling. By using Ouch, you are teaching the dog that humans are much easier to hurt and that they must play easier with people than they can with another dog.

All of these "Problem Behaviors" come from the dog wanting to either play or to get something you have. In both cases, the answer lies in teaching patience and impulse control. "Gentle", "Wait" and "Ouch" will require practice and time to become reliable, so don't get mad or impatient. Get smart and get in there and start teaching! This just might be a skill that could save this shelter animal!

13

TOUCH SENSITIVITY

The topic of touch sensitivity has a lot to do with reactivity. You must understand that to most dogs, anything new is something scary, and that alone can create a dog who does not like being touched. Combine this knowledge with the fact that a dog's social developmental period, or the time where we can affect whether the world is scary or fun, is very short...starting around weeks 3 to 4 and ending around weeks 18 to 20. If dogs are not allowed or do not get the chance to experience the world in a positive way, they are likely to end up with shy, nervous or anxious personalities. Equate this to the shelter world and dogs coming into a shelter after the age of 4-5 months will have their personality already set...

Think of it this way...in a relationship or marriage, people learn very quickly that changing one's spouse or significant other's personality is virtually impossible. We can however, work on specific behaviors and possibly change those. As an example, my wife has trained me to pick up my socks every evening. But she would be the first to tell you that it has not expanded to my general tidiness around the rest of the house! Behaviors can be changed, personalities cannot!

So, just what do we do? We work with Fido and introduce ideas relating to specific behaviors using counter conditioning and operant conditioning. We use lots of repetitions and associate something awesome (typically treats and other things the dog loves) with the scary things, thus making them more appealing, or at least more pleasant to be around! Unfortunately this process is, at best, very time consuming and in many cases something that has to be continued throughout the life of the animal.

In other cases where counter conditioning does not work (or work fast enough) we must leave the world of training and enter the world of management. In other words, we focus primarily on making the dog, its environment and the people around it safe. For those who have dealt with this situation, it is a 24/7 job that can never be relaxed or ended. Sadly, in many shelter cases, these dogs are simply euthanized for triage reasons and also since it makes more sense to spend resources on dogs that are easier to adopt. This is the part of my job I truly hate... evaluating a dog, realizing the dog is a danger to society and that unless we can find a professional dog trainer to adopt the dog, that reentry into society is, well unfair and unethical to not only people but the dog as well. The hardest part of the decision is the realization that the only reason the dog is a danger to society is the fact that society failed the dog. Relax... I am not giving up that easy!

So just what is it we can do with those rescue/shelter dogs where the damage has already been done? This is the reason I preach, beg, plead and teach the idea of puppy training. You only get one chance (and such a small period of time) to introduce and teach a puppy that the world is not only safe and fun, but it is good to enjoy with people and other animals. Waste that chance, and a dog with touch sensitivity is a distinct possibility. Unfortunately, dogs with touch sensitivity many times end up biting. And we know biters have a very slim chance of getting out of a shelter alive so let's get down to how to help them…

We will start with a definition of touch sensitivity or what it looks like in a shelter dog or your own dog at home. It is a dog or animal who fears or is uncomfortable with being touched in certain areas. For dogs, the usual "hot spots" are

- Ears
- Mouth
- Feet
- Tail
- Private Parts

Don't believe me? Ask your local groomer how many bites or snarky behaviors they have seen as a result of touching one or all of these areas! This is the reason the American Kennel Club includes these areas in the Canine Good Citizen certification test. Trust me, it is very important for dogs to realize that touch by humans is a good thing and not at all something scary. If you have found yourself with an older dog joining the family, or you volunteer in a shelter, this just may be a behavior you have or will encounter. The question is how do we deal with it, and just what are we supposed to do? The answer is a technique called Cradle and Massage.

For lack of a better term, it is therapeutic massage for pooches. Ideally we want a dog that will willingly lie on its back in your lap, let you pet them, massage their ears and feet, look at their teeth, and touch the tail and private parts, in other words...love human touch. Keep in mind that this is an end goal, not what we should ever expect from a dog on day one of handling.

We start by simply sitting on the floor with a bag of dog food and hand feeding the dog! I actually ask my clients to hand feed their dogs for at least the first 30 days they are in the family. This process really jump starts the bonding period with your dog, teaches dogs to be careful around human hands and conveys the message that we humans are pretty damn important (without needing to be a jerk) to the dog! I know it sounds crazy, but I challenge you to try the 30 day hand feed and see the results for yourself. You will soon have a dog that looks at you as the "pack leader" (man I hate that saying), but it is because Fido needs you rather than is being dominated by you.

Now back to cradle and massage...as you are feeding the dog, you pay for the touch; touch an ear get some food, quick touch of a paw more food. GO SLOW! If you go too fast, you will just end up making the situation worse, and will wind up giving the dog another reason to be fearful. In my opinion, techniques like this need to begin under the watchful eye of a good dog trainer if the dog is already showing touch sensitivity, but with your average dog or puppy this is something everyone should try!

As the dog becomes more comfortable being touched (after all we are paying per touch, right?), we are going to teach him a trick..."Roll Over". It is fun, easy and a great way to get a dog to roll over on his side or back and allow you to pet and touch without being as fearful. A word of caution about "down" and "roll over"...both are extremely submissive positions for a dog to offer, and if they don't appear to want to offer the position, DO NOT FORCE IT!!! You have probably moved too fast and the dog is nervous, anxious or just not ready. Simply go back to hand feeding, allowing the dog to relax and build trust. A great way to think about any counter conditioning or operant conditioning is to always reward dogs for being brave and never give them a reason to be fearful. It seems simple and trust me; it is rule #1 in my book for dog training!

Training Tip:
Don't be that silly person who says "Don't worry I am a dog person" right before you force yourself on a dog, only to leave this world with fewer fingers than you entered with...

Back to rollover; it is as simple as luring a dog (while enjoying their massage) from a down, using a treat, to roll over to their side so you can rub their belly. Go **slow** and eventually you will be able to get the dog to roll all the way over! As we achieve "roll over" and continue the idea of cradle and massage (treats for touch), we can introduce different environments in which to play this game. We can even introduce additional people to the party, having one feed while the other touches or even including different types of people; gender, race, old and young. The more ways and angles we can send to the dog with the message that touch is a good thing and not a scary thing the better off we are. Just remember, it has taken Fido his entire life to mistrust touch and/or people. You, as the volunteer, must be patient enough to allow him to work out his issues on his own time table not yours or the shelters!

I like to think of these dogs as people with personal space issues (we all know someone with these issues) and realize that trying to fix it by telling someone to walk up and give them a big hug or a sloppy kiss, is probably not going to work! Go slow and always remember: ***Only give reasons to be brave, never reasons to be afraid,*** and before you know it you will start to see a braver, more confident and even more important, an adoptable dog.

14

HYPERACTIVITY

Last but not least, let's talk about hyperactivity! I am really hoping at this point you can almost guess what we are going to talk about now, but if not, here are the main topics

❊ Exercise
❊ Impulse Control
❊ Non negotiable Rules

Face it, a hyper dog in a home or shelter environment is not unusual; it may be completely normal for the type of life they are living. The same could be said for a 9 year old who never gets gym class or recess. They are allowed (or left no other choice) to act out due to the fact they have been given no rules or routines in which to live by. What specific behaviors would you expect from the child I just described? Would you expect a perfect little angel? If not, then why do most humans expect a shelter or family dog to just "be good"? Hopefully described this way, you can see it doesn't make much sense does it? Remember, my dog training business is called Keep it Simple

Stupid Dog Training for a reason. So let's get down to helping the four legged goon you are dealing with!

In my experience there are two types of shelter organizations. First you have the ones with crazy, out of control dogs that are never allowed to interact with other dogs (or people for that matter). These are the shelters that constantly say they don't have the staff (either in number or experience) or the resources to do anything different. They live with the false hope that something miraculous is going to happen and that everything will work out in the end, just because they care about the animals.

The other shelter organizations hire the best employees, try new things and are on the cutting edge of training their volunteers. If you are in the second group, this book was not written for you, (but I hope you are enjoying it)!

To the first group I leave you with the same message I give my clients that don't put in the time to train their dogs, and are frustrated with their results...

"DOING THE SAME THING OVER AND OVER AND EXPECTING DIFFERENT RESULTS IS THE DEFINITION OF CRAZY" AND I CAN NOT HELP YOU UNTIL YOU REALIZE IT!!!

You are going to have to look at the idea of color coding your volunteers (discussed in more detail in chapter 15) as well as introducing the idea of play groups. You need to hire an experienced shelter manager (one who can control the situation and not just love the dogs). Will it be easy? NO. Will you make mistakes? YES. Over time, will the plight and condition of your shelter dogs improve? YES. Now don't get me wrong...not all dogs will play nice with others, but do not try and tell me there are not at least 5-10 dogs in your shelter right now that would do fine together in a play group!

So, the best place to start is with exercise!

The end result of this rant is that "a tired dog is a good dog" and that thinking an out of control walk by an untrained volunteer once or twice a week will fix the issue is just plain silly. For those of you reading this book looking for help with their own dog, go find a reliable doggy day care in your area. Talk to them and listen to them about whether your dog is cut out for such a program. Trust me, if Fido is, it might be the best decision you ever make!

For those of you who are volunteers at a shelter that is in the first category and not utilizing these ideas, bang this drum till your shelter listens. I know you think there are tons of reasons for why it won't work, I am just asking you to find the one reason that will make it work, with the wonderful result of more dogs being adopted into their FOREVER HOMES!

Now it's time to discuss impulse control. Impulse control is something that every parent and dog owner in the world understands. It amazes me that more people don't see the similarities in dealing with both dogs and young children!

The idea of "ignore the bad and reward the good" means insisting on a clear set of rules (such as sit, say please), and realizing that yelling and screaming only makes situations worse. Because it is so simple, I think we just tend to overlook the obvious. The entire idea is so easy, just teach them that they need to be patient and in most cases they will get what they want. Think of it like this, "If I get what I want, then you will get what you want".

Remember lining up in the fourth grade to go to lunch, recess or anywhere outside of the classroom, and learning that until everyone was in a straight line and quiet we could not go? It takes a while to get everyone to learn the need to follow these rules, I guarantee that it did not happen the first week of school, and likely not in the first month of school! It takes a while for fourth graders to learn impulse control as well. The same is true when training a dog. You won't be perfect after a 6 week training class, or after one or two session of working with a shelter dog. My suggestion and advice for you is to relax, have some fun and remember to "Keep it Simple Stupid"! For those of us that still have children living under our roof, we realize that we are constantly in a teaching and coaching roll. Heck, even those of us whose kids that have left the nest are still coaching and teaching! Dogs, especially younger ones, have issues with impulse control. Don't expect more out of your dog than you did your child. Instead, why not try working as hard with your dog as you did with your child? Chances are, it will go much faster. And if you are thinking that this sounds like way too much work, then I suggest you consider a goldfish, not a dog, as a pet , or find a different type of volunteer organization to work with. (Sorry but the truth hurts sometimes).

Lastly, I want to share the idea of non-negotiable rules. Go into the shelter every day the same way, expect the same thing, work on the same behaviors and focus on things you know will get the dogs adopted! You and I both know people want dogs that know how to "sit". They want dogs that are social with people and other dogs. They want dogs that can walk nicely on a leash. Why waste your time dealing with things you cannot change or fix? The key is to be consistent and stop sending the dog mixed messages; today it is ok to jump on me, yesterday it was not. Pulling on the leash is ok when I am listening to my iPod but when I am paying attention to you it is not. Have a plan and work the plan. It does not matter if you are working in a shelter or are trying to train your own dog, pick your non-negotiable rules and make them your daily routine! If you think about it, every example I have given you in this book has to do with exercise, impulse control, and the lack of routines and rules. We are the ones screwing up the dogs by giving them too much freedom and not letting them know exactly what we want. Hey I did not promise a magic pill or a super-secret trick! There is only one way to fix problem behaviors or to train a dog. We start by setting rules, establishing routines, rewarding the behaviors we like and ignoring the behaviors we don't! It is no more complicated than that. The question is...are you willing to do the work to bring these changes to your shelter or home?

15

WHAT CAN VOLUNTEERS REALLY DO TO HELP?

Ok, so we finally get to the chapter that started the entire idea for this book. Just what should volunteers do when they show up at the shelter and want to help? The first thing that must happen is to change the way most shelters handle their volunteers! Most volunteers get very little actual training, and in many cases are just pointed to where the dogs are housed and told good luck. This leads to volunteers choosing dogs that they cannot handle, to dogs being taught (and learning) bad habits and in many cases creating dogs that are not adoptable. On top of that, many shelters are short-handed and lack sufficient funding. This puts a ton of pressure on an already exhausted management team just trying to survive. So...this is usually the point where someone says "There is nothing else possible that can be done to improve this situation!" But I believe there is a solution; one that I brought up earlier...the idea of categorizing dogs with red, yellow and green colors so that volunteers and staff will have a better idea of which dogs could possibly be together, all done using the "Stoplight Method". The basic idea is as follows...

❋ Red Dogs play alone...period; they do not play well with others.
❋ Yellow Dogs only play with other yellow dogs; they are too shy and under socialized to relate with high energy dogs.
❋ Green Dogs are the social butterflies that love playing with everyone. Many puppies, which will grow into green dogs if given the chance, fall into this category. They deserve the right, freedom and reward to play.

I then want to take this idea to the next level... a volunteer training program! It is important that volunteers be given the tools to succeed!!! So, we are not only going to categorize the dogs, but also categorize the volunteers. If you are a well-trained and experienced volunteer, you will have a red categorization which means you can work with red dogs as well as yellow and green dogs. Those folks who have only some experience and training would have a yellow categorization which means they would only deal with yellow and green dogs. Those volunteers who are new or are not as dog savvy would have the green categorization and only deal with green dogs. This simple idea will not only help keep volunteers safe, but will also make sure the dogs are getting the best care and support they can receive.

Yes, the shelter will have to set up and administer the training. I have found that doing a seminar type presentation, followed by a hands-on session, is the easiest and most time effective way to get started. This way you have waves of volunteers moving up the ranks. If we don't create structure, then the volunteers are going to continue inadvertently teaching bad behaviors and that is going to equate to fewer adoptions and to more dogs losing their lives. Without this training, there is also a higher likelihood of volunteers getting hurt by doing something they are not capable of or are not trained to attempt. So, let's do what is right, and go buy some green, yellow and red stickers for the dogs and some green, yellow and red file folders for the volunteers and get busy.

Now for the specifics... what do I think the roles of volunteers should be? Well, in my opinion, there should be three types of volunteers in every shelter and they are...

❉ Readers (Green/Yellow Volunteers)
❉ Groomers (Yellow/Red Volunteers)
❉ Walkers (Yellow/Red Volunteers)

In the past, training I have done with shelters is usually broken down into sections something like this...

❉ Level one training (green volunteers) is a seminar covering Basic Positive Reinforcement Training, Problem Behaviors and Basic Dog Body Language. This also includes an introduction to the READER and GROOMER Positions. It is then followed up by a "hands on" class covering the "how to" on these topics.

❉ Level two training (yellow volunteers) is a much more in depth discussion and video presentation of dog body language including a discussion of how to use counter conditioning and rewards to change behavior. This also includes an introduction to the WALKER position. This level is only a seminar with a question and answer period.

✳ Level three training (red) is the "how to" of administering dog intake evaluations and what to look for when doing the evaluations. This level is part video, part question and answer and part "hands on".

I will also have specific continuing education seminars for all levels dealing with specific problem behaviors, such as those we covered in the earlier chapters of this book. When you get right down to it, you will have to commit to 1-3 training sessions per month to adequately get volunteers up to speed and trained appropriately!

As crazy as these three positions may sound, I promise to break down each one, and talk specifically about what each does, as well as discuss the changes these positions will bring about in the dogs as we try to find their forever homes! By the time you understand all three positions, I hope you will have an A-Ha moment about how easy it will be to change the shelter environment. And you can do this by not only having well trained volunteers, but also by realizing that taking a dog for a walk is hardly the most important thing a volunteer can do!

16

VOLUNTEERS AS READERS

Have you ever walked into your local shelter and been greeted by a wall of noise...all of the barking, growling, and howling in one, huge, eardrum breaking sound? Now ask yourself, how many people that are looking for dogs and then hear all of that noise, turn right around and leave the shelter without further consideration of adopting a dog?

In previous chapters we have talked about the importance of socialization in dogs, how anxiety can create problem behaviors like barking, and even how dogs who were never taught to like being around people are fearful and thus trigger barking. The good news is that if you introduce a reader position within the volunteer ranks, it can and will help fix this problem. Read on and find out how.

Readers will work in three basic environments:

1. The shelter itself
2. Outside on a leash or outdoor kennel
3. The quiet/isolation room

Let's start in the shelter itself. The goal of a "Reader" is simple; getting dogs used to being around people and to get them to be calm/quiet when they see people. The first thing a reader is going to do inside the shelter is grab a folding chair, a book or newspaper, sit down and start reading. The reader is to completely ignore all of the barking, whining and growling they hear and just read. As the minutes go by, the dogs are going to realize something new is happening. This person sitting here in my kennel area is not looking at me, talking to me or 'please no', walking up to the kennel or cage and looking at me! Very quickly, the dogs are going to figure out that barking doesn't get them any reaction whatsoever and that there is no real reason to continue. They might resort to some other behavior instead of barking, such as jumping up on the kennel doors or spinning in circles or pacing. But in the end, the dogs begin to realize that all of this commotion is really a waste of time since it is not getting them anything, so they might as well stop. We are going to slowly but surely condition the dogs to the fact that the presence of people is normal and nothing for them to get worked up over. The next step is to begin adding an alternative behavior that we can start rewarding, in addition to ignoring the barking.

So, just what is that alternative behavior going to be? Yep, you guessed it... "SIT". Our goal here is to give no attention whatsoever to the barking, thus making the behavior unrewarding. At the same time we are adding the desirable behavior of "sit", which we can reward! After all, what self-respecting dog will waste energy doing something that gets them nothing? Pair that with a new behavior that gets us a reward and you are on your way to a much quieter kennel! Now ask yourself a simple question, "Which dog will get adopted faster the barker or the dog who sits?" Now that you understand what we are trying to accomplish, let's discuss the "how to" of this equation.

Let's say the volunteer is there for an hour. They have their book or magazine, their chair and they are actively reading and ignoring the dogs. I now want the volunteer to stop at least three times an hour and walk through the kennel. However, I do not want them to look at, talk to or otherwise communicate with the dogs in any way. Rather, I want them to keep a watch from the corner of their eye at each kennel door, pause and wait, let's say for 20-30 seconds.

Now our end goal is a quiet, sitting dog, but to expect this right off the bat is unfair. So in the beginning, we might only get a dog that stops barking at you, or maybe they are sitting but still barking. Either way if something good (sitting or quiet) happens, the reader tosses a treat in the kennel and moves to the next one. In dog training we call this shaping a behavior. We are accepting a partially correct response and rewarding it so that the next time we can delay the reward and get a little closer to what we really want. If the dog does not quit barking or sit, the choice is simple, move on to the next kennel. After going through all the kennels, the reader goes back to the chair for another chapter of reading (or about 20 minutes) then repeats the process. Try by try, hour by hour and day by day you are going to see less barking and more sitting. The reason…the dogs are simply learning by association that barking and crazy gets us nothing, while being quiet and sitting gets us a cookie!

At the same time, we are desensitizing the dog to the presence of people. Honestly, the more readers you can have in the kennel at once the better. This way the dogs get used to more than just one person being present. Another thing to consider is the ability that dogs have of learning from each other. Trust me; the noisy ones are going to start putting together why George in the kennel next door keeps getting all the treats! No matter what angle we look at the reader position from, we have begun to teach the dogs that certain behaviors are rewarded while others are ignored and therefore not worth continuing.

Obviously, the reading position is the perfect position for our green volunteers. This is a way of volunteering that requires very little training and/or management. But don't get me wrong, I honestly think these folks are going to be the ones that create the biggest change in the dogs at any shelter! So treat 'em good and take the time to explain the process to them so they buy into the idea. After all, they are your front line in the war to get more dogs adopted!

How about taking a dog out on a nice day and just sitting under a tree and reading a book? My whole goal with the idea of readers is to create dogs that are okay being around people and not having to be attended to or being pushy about getting our attention. Dogs, like people, must realize at some point in their life that some periods of quiet are necessary to be balanced. It also helps dogs to become independent! Face it, dogs at some point in their life will have to be alone for a period of time, and those dogs that have human interaction and attention 24/7 become what I call Velcro Dogs. Those are the dogs that have to be around their owner all the time or they break down. Some even enter the world of separation anxiety and that, my friends, is a terrible thing to witness. Remember that down time, alone time and independence are all things dogs need, to be balanced. Unfortunately, this again is where our humanness gets in the way. We feel the need to hold, cuddle and make everything better by giving into every request for attention. I don't want you to think that giving your dog attention is a bad thing, but rather that dogs should give us appropriate behaviors that we then reward with our attention. Think of your attention as the paycheck and the behavior we want from our dog as the work!

Now don't think the green volunteers get all the fun here… there are plenty of opportunities for more seasoned red and yellow volunteers to use this same technique. For example, what if a particular dog is scared of, anxious or even possibly snippy around people? In that case why not have a seasoned volunteer start a desensitization program with the dog using the reading method. Start with the reader sitting outside the dog's kennel and just reading. Rewards come as the dog investigates or is quiet around the person. You could then graduate to removal of the chair and have the person sit right in front of the kennel, on the ground, still outside the kennel, but close enough so that the dog can start to sniff the stranger. All the while, the dog is learning that this person is not scary and is in fact someone who will reward the dog being brave, allowing the dog to investigate at their own pace, and growing more confident and relaxed. The next stage might be reading in a "quiet room" where the dog is loose along with the reader who still at this point is ignoring the dog, waiting for that glorious moment when the dog comes up and investigates the person and is rewarded with a treat! Of course treats are given during the entire process. The key here is to let the dog grow braver and then reward the appropriate behaviors. Our only job is to ignore the dog, allowing the dog to progress at his own pace, gaining confidence and CHOOSING to progress. That being said, a very dog savvy person is required in these instances, typically red volunteers and occasionally some very strong yellow volunteers.

Now we will discuss volunteers as groomers.

17

VOLUNTEERS AS GROOMERS

If Readers are all helping dogs having positive associations about being around people, then Groomers are all about dogs having positive associations with human touch. Groomers are not going to be new volunteers, but instead should be those folks who are comfortable handling dogs and who are also accomplished at reading the body language of dogs. Any dog that is going to live with humans must know that human touch is a good thing and it has rewards. Ask trainers, veterinarians and dog groomers how many times and why they have been bitten, and it will become readily apparent that there are several "hot spots" or areas on a dog where, without work, they are just not comfortable being handled or touched. A general list of these spots would include; feet, mouth, tail, ears, private areas and their own collar. My goal is to have volunteers in every shelter whose job it is to just sit with the dogs, once again in that "quiet room", and allow the dog to learn to tolerate, accept and eventually enjoy the touch of a human. As with the last section, treats are going to play a big role in this. In many cases, grooming volunteers are going to start out the same way as readers, with a book and ignoring the dog! As the dog gains confidence and is investigating the groomer, via sniffing or engaging the person in touch, treats are going to be given to reward that bravery and to reinforce the fact that touch is a good thing. The next step will be putting one's hand on the ground and allowing the dog to sniff and investigate the hand without fear of it moving. With each sniff the hand releases a treat.

Once we have the trust and comfort of the dog, we will make the first attempt at touch. A word of caution here, dogs do not naturally like being patted on top of the head! Think about it, how would you like someone thumping you on top of the head? Instead, you should, WITH ALL DOGS, start with a gentle touch under the chin. Think of it as a soft gentle caress under the chin (I don't know about you but this seems a lot more enjoyable!) and after every touch; yep Fido gets a treat. This is not an overnight fix. Just to give perspective; some dogs might take weeks if not months just to get to this point. This is also the reason that I think the grooming volunteers inside shelters should be folks with plenty of experience around dogs! Trust me, if you don't know what you are doing, it is likely you will leave this world with fewer fingers than you entered with, have a dog even more scared of people, and YOU will have been the reason. That being said... off my soapbox and to the next step of skills needed to be a Groomer.

Just as slowly, we are going to add feet, mouth, tail, ears, belly, private parts and even the dog's own collar. Of course, after each individual touch what will follow... yep Fido gets that delicious treat! I want Fido to be excited to have his paw touched by anybody because he knows he is going to get a yummy treat.

Speaking of hot spots, did you know a large percentage of dog bites come directly or indirectly in connection to grabbing a dog's collar? This is why I add the collar as one of the areas of focus. A dog who knows that getting his collar grabbed means he has a chance for a treat won't be part of those statistics. Likewise, dogs that learn good things happen when humans touch me are going to stand a much better chance of not only getting adopted but staying that way!

Other things that the Groomers are going to be working on are actually using brushes, combs, nail trimmers and all sorts of other tools around the dogs and on them. Keep in mind, while all of these ideas sound great and might really make sense, the one thing that folks always get wrong is the time involved. This process can take months and months of daily counter conditioning. (Fancy words for making something that is scary become fun or rewarding!) The sessions for groomers will also be way shorter as compared with the readers. Whereas a reader can go for an hour plus reading away, groomers will very likely only work 10-15 minutes per session in the beginning and YOU MUST WORK SLOWLY AND KNOW WHEN THE DOG IS GOING INTO THE STRESS ZONE AND STOP. This is not a quick fix or an easy one. Think of it this way, the slower you go, the better learned the skills will be from the dog's perspective!!!!

The next step in this process is what I call cradle and massage. Think of it like therapeutic massage for dogs. Just get the dog to lie down near you and begin rubbing the ears, the muzzle, face, and feet...you name it! I want the goal here to be a totally relaxed dog enjoying a rub down by a human. Once again, the idea is for the dog to enjoy and to look forward to human touch. A dog that has learned this life lesson is going to be way easier to adopt and will also be way less likely to ever have issues that get it brought back to the shelter!

Now we have a dog that is OK around people and even OK being touched by people. So, what else can we do as shelter volunteers? This is where the walkers come in. The dog is ready for a walk, since not only is he social about being around people, but he even likes being touched. I am hoping that you are realizing that many of the dogs that volunteers have been walking are nowhere near ready to be walked. Dogs that are not calm around people and enjoy being handled and/or touched by humans are not ready for the high energy activity of going for a walk. In many cases, the first thing a volunteer wants to do is grab a leash and get dragged all over the neighborhood! I hope you are coming to grips with the idea that by walking them in an uncontrollable manner, you are making things worse. No worries though, because that is the next thing we are going to learn...how to take this newly formed social and friendly dog and teach them how to walk nicely on a leash!

18

VOLUNTEERS AS WALKERS

Don't get me wrong...calm, social and easy-going or not, shelter dogs (and pet dogs) must get exercise. For the most part, that means getting to go on a walk. However, it also means they need to get out in the exercise yard. As I mentioned in an earlier chapter, we also need to work on socialization and brain work with shelter dogs and pet dogs. This, again, is the main reason that I have to remind you...new volunteers should not be walking dogs! This is the one experience that can undermine all of the hard work the readers and groomers are attempting to make happen. Think about it, you put an out-of-control or manipulative (one who has figured out how to push buttons) dog along with a volunteer who has no idea how to handle problem behaviors for a walk, and ask yourself, just what kind of behavior is being reinforced? Let me give you a couple of examples.

The Dog Who Pulls on the Leash:

Well there are three common mistakes that new or inexperienced volunteers make. They are yelling, touching/tugging and/or allowing the walk to continue.

Let's start with the yelling. While the dog is pulling the volunteer's arm out of the socket, the volunteer starts yelling NO, SIT, STOP or even begins cussing the dog. Now, I hate to be the one to break the news to everyone, but dogs do not speak English; and when we start yelling and screaming at them, all that registers to the dog is "Wow... listen to Mom or Dad, they are barking at me, isn't this a fun game?" Depending on your relationship with the dog, it is likely going to excite them even more. This does nothing but increase the pull or it scares the dog which still increases the pull, but more so because the dog is now trying to get away from the lunatic at the other end of the leash. The end result is that yelling does not work.

Touching/tugging is a mistake that means nothing more than in most cases, attempts at corrections or punishments. Unfortunately, most new volunteers think this works. And they saw it on TV, so why wouldn't it work, right? The most common of these mistakes is the leash correction or the old jerk & pop. Let's really look at this situation. What is it we are trying to stop? Simple – we want to stop the pulling on the leash or put a different way, we want the leash to be loose. So, let me ask you a question... can you jerk a dog's leash when the leash is already tight? Of course not, you can only jerk or use a leash pop if there is slack in the leash. So here is the scenario... the dog is dragging you down the sidewalk, all the while you are patiently waiting for your chance to pop the leash. Finally, Fido slows down and there is enough slack in the leash for you to jerk the leash. Guess what just happened... you just corrected your dog for having a loose leash! Yep I said it, your dog finally gave you what you wanted and you just jerked the crap out of him! Even if you jerk prior to the pull, you are still correcting a loose leash, not a tight leash. Fido starts to realize that if the leash is tight, which in reality means pulling, everything is good and no correction is happening. But if he slows down and allows the leash to go slack, he gets jerked and/or corrected. As you can see, this is exactly the opposite of what we want!

The final mistake we are going to talk about is allowing the pulling to happen. You are probably thinking to yourself "Does this fool think I want this to happen?" Let's again look at it from Fido's point of view. We know that dogs will only continue behaviors that are rewarding or that get them what they want; otherwise there would be no reason to engage in the behavior, right? By letting Fido pull, you are inadvertently rewarding Fido by allowing him to have access to whatever he is pulling you toward. Think of it this way, "When a dog is walking, what is the reward to the dog?" Well, it is simply the walk itself. Dogs enjoy going on a walk; smelling, seeing, hearing and experiencing the world. They could care less about whether they are walking nicely or saving time by dragging you to where they want to go. So by allowing the walk to continue while Fido's behavior (pulling) is happening, you are rewarding this pulling behavior. Hopefully you can now see how important it is for volunteers to understand dogs and dog behavior, before being turned loose with a dog. If not, all the work the readers and groomers have been putting in is for naught, since the dogs are being re-taught to be crazy each and every time they get to go for a walk.

So just what is it our walkers should be doing to correct the crazy out of control walks? I would start with two techniques.

The first is the simplest idea of all - if the dog pulls...STOP and wait. The walk will not begin again until the dog is calm and sitting! This is an idea that must be 100% consistent across volunteers. If not, your one bad apple (volunteer that allows the pull) will ruin the entire process. Dogs need consistency to learn and to expect anything different is silly! I make this distinction so that it is very clear...a dependable and regular volunteer is not the same as an "educated" volunteer. That volunteer that comes every day no matter what, that feels the dogs should be allowed to do whatever they want because they need the exercise, or because being outside their kennel is in the end more important than leash skills, is NOT helping. In fact, I would counter that volunteers that allow those behaviors will create dogs that spend their entire life in a shelter, or may even be sentenced to death, because they are so out of control...making them incapable of finding their forever home.

On top of the STOP idea, we must also teach a strong and reliable "watch me" command. This was covered in detail in Chapter 11: Pulling on the Leash. Now keep in mind, this can take some time, so be patient and just wait. If Fido just doesn't get it, go back to working on your "watch me" until it is more automatic and then try again. Ask for a "watch me", turn your back and take one giant step in any direction, then stop and wait. Fido will come around front, sit and look at you. Don't forget to treat or praise here. It doesn't have to always be food, but you do have to give Fido some form of reward. Again, take a step in another direction and wait. You are on your way to teaching the dog what I refer to as an "auto sit". If the walker stops for any reason, the dog's job is to come to the front, sit, look at the walker and wait for the next move. Obviously as we progress, one step becomes two and two becomes three. Once you reach a reliability of around 10 steps we are ready to add the leash! Yep that's right, we don't start with a leash or outdoors but that's the next step. Keep in mind that when we go outdoors from indoors or from an exercise yard, we start completely over. Once again starting with just "watch me", then turning our backs, then adding steps and so on. The only difference is that you now have a leash on the dog. As you progress, you keep adding distractions; people, other dogs, squirrels or whatever else you can experience. Over time using the "Stop" and the "Don't turn your back on me" techniques will produce a dog that can and will walk nicely on a leash as long as the walker understands what to do when pulling occurs. I know this sounds crazy, but most experienced trainers realize the best response to a problem behavior is absolutely nothing. It's better to wait for Fido to choose correctly so that we can reinforce the good behavior and increase the chance of it happening again.

19

DOG AS A SECOND LANGUAGE (DASL)

This brings us to the last chapter of "how-to" stuff before we conclude. In many ways it is the most important chapter. It has to do with safety and how to prevent getting ourselves, other people or volunteers hurt. I like to refer to the following ideas as "Dog as a Second Language" or DASL. Put simply, it's how we read canine body language to try to understand when dogs are nervous, anxious, scared, aggressive or happy. This, above all else, is what differentiates a good volunteer from a great volunteer. While this skill can be taught, (that is what this chapter is all about) I do feel that certain people come by this knowledge naturally, and can read body language with little, if any, teaching. If you have volunteers like this, cherish them and treat them well. They will become the lifeblood in your shelter. Outside of the kennel, point them to a local trainer to mentor them. Trust me...we need all the great dog trainers we can get!

So let's get started on our road to learning DASL. We are going to focus on what are referred to as calming signals. This is the body language or behaviors/actions that dogs use to tell humans and other dogs that they are not comfortable, and that things need to slow down. The reason we are going to focus on calming signals is simple. Whether dog, cat, monkey or person, an individual who is fearful or anxious has only three ways to deal with stress of any kind…freeze, flight and fight. And as you see, they build in severity as the stressor increases. The scenario might go something like this. Dog A, unbeknownst to a shelter, is fearful or uncomfortable around men in hats. Fred, a new volunteer, loves dogs and decides he is going to walk this dog. As Fred walks up to Dog A wearing his favorite baseball cap, he does not notice that Dog A stops moving in his kennel and looks away from Fred. He then goes inside the cage and Dog A quickly moves to the back of the kennel continuing to look away, but now starting to lick his lips. Fred also fails to see that Dog A has his tail tucked between his legs because Dog A is in a sitting position. Fred then tries to put the leash on Dog A and the dog lashes out biting Fred several times in quick succession causing a nasty injury that requires 4 stitches! Dog A did everything a dog knows how to do to let another dog know he was scared. He quit moving and looked away, he tried to get away, and still looking away he even had his tail between his legs. Any dog on the planet would have known to slow their approach and wait for Dog A to make the first move, but Fred, not knowing how to speak DASL, has inadvertently gotten hurt, probably caused the shelter's workman's comp insurance to increase and, depending on the shelter, might well have put Dog A on death row, all due to Fred's lack of experience and knowledge. So let's get on with learning DASL and making sure everyone is safe and smart!

Before I talk about any specific body language examples, let me be clear that the only appropriate response to a calming signal is to stop moving, look away from the dog and slowly move back until you see the body language relax. Doing anything else is cruel. Plus, it only gives the dog more reasons to be scared of a particular stimulus (guys in hats, sunglasses, deep voices or anything else new). The fact of the matter is, to a dog, anything new is at first scary. Unless we pair the new thing with something good (treats or food) or the dog is allowed to encounter the new thing on the dog's terms (i.e. Dog coming to person once comfortable; not the person going to the dog), it remains scary. Trust me, if we don't do this pairing, the freeze, flight and fight process will begin. Keep in mind that I am describing juvenile and adult dogs outside of the social developmental period. Puppies are a different ball game, and you can teach them to be very confident; however they still scare and hold fears very easily. It is our job to do two things.

1.   Make every experience positive and not scary, by pairing it with something positive and/or yummy. All children give the dog canned chicken or hot dogs so the dog learns being around kids is an awesome experience!

2.   Learn to read dog body language so that you can tell when fear and anxiety are present. Slow down the process to allow the dog the opportunity to choose to be brave and to make the first move, then simply begin pairing the process with food and/or praise.

Hopefully you are starting to understand what I want you to do, but we still need to cover how. In other words...I need to teach you how to read a dog's calming signals and to become fluent in DASL. So let's get started!

Here is a list and a brief explanation of several behaviors that will let you know you are moving **way** too fast and that you need to slow down and let the dog recover before proceeding.

❋ Dog Suddenly Freezes - "Oh crap! Don't move and maybe this scary thing won't see me!" Slow down, stop and ignore the dog. Maybe take a step or two back and wait for the dog to relax. My suggestion is to wait for the dog to come to you, and at the very least, wait on moving forward again until the dog is relaxed. Go at Fido's pace not yours.

❋ Dog Tries to Run or Avoid You – "You are not going to hurt me since I can run faster than you can!" Once again, just sit down and ignore the dog. It's the only way to convince the dog you are not after him.

❋ Dog Yawns – This one is an auto signal similar to us chewing our nails or wringing our hands when we are nervous. If you are smart enough to know this about a stranger, then realizing the same for a dog should not be a huge leap. Slow down and let Fido make the first move

❋ Dog is Licking his Lips – This is another auto behavior that shows anxiety. "I am not sure what is going to happen next and I really don't like it!" Relax…you're a volunteer. You are not getting paid by the hour, so just take your time.

❋ Dog's Tail is Between his Legs – This one comes after or along with one of the auto behaviors, and it is simply one more signal Fido is trying to send to this dense human who keeps bothering him. You are moving too fast and Fido doesn't yet trust you. Do you think continuing to try and touch the dog is gonna fix this?

❋ Excessive Scratching of themselves – "La La La I don't see you, the scary thing isn't really there. I just know when I look up it will be gone!" Really... you think that trying to get closer to this dog is a good thing? Why not stop in your tracks or back up and maybe throw some yummy treats in the dog's direction?

❋ Chewing on their Feet – Same story, different behavior or signal. "I can't hear you, you are not really there!" Once again, try treats from a distance and then ignore. As the dog gains confidence, he will decide to investigate you. Reward his bravery and don't make him more scared.

❋ Continual Licking - "OK, I am going to take a bath and clean myself and by the time I am done the scary person will be gone!" This would be a great time to have a seat and grab a book and just become a reader. This gives Fido a chance to choose to say hello rather than for us to try to force it.

❋ Ears flattened or Pinned back – "I have warned you once, and trust me I am not going to do it again!" Just stop moving and wait for the dog to relax. You should also stop making direct eye contact.

❋ Hair on the dog's back is up (hackles) - This one is usually not one that is an "I am scared" or an "uncomfortable" signal. Rather it is usually a laser-like focus on something or someone (dog or human.) In this case, I would rethink the plan I am following and reset, because the dog is too stimu-lated to continue. (A side note on hackling... some dogs even do this during play, but be wary of what is going on if you do not personally know the dog!) ($0.25 word - the scientific word for this is pileo-erection!)

* Urination Upon Being Touched – Have you ever seen a movie where someone is so scared they lose control of their bladder? Well guess what...you have just done the same thing to this poor dog. Do you think you should back up or just keep pushing?

* Constant shaking off (similar to what your dog does during and after a bath!) This is another behavior designed to show the dog is uncomfortable. Something you are doing is making Fido nervous! Just slow down and allow the dog to recover before continuing!

* Loose Stools – Ever heard of the saying "So scared I just %*@# my pants!"? This one ought to be pretty damn obvious! Slow down or maybe even leave the area. This dog might be a good candidate for a chair outside the kennel and a reader, rather than torturing the poor dog...

* Smell (Releasing Anal Glands) - This can happen right before the dog defecates on the floor or as simply a reaction to stress. Dogs have glands on either side of the anus that secret a smell that is their calling card to other dogs, but they can also completely release them when they are extremely scared. It smells like poop but different, in a weird way. Let's just say you will know when it happens, and if you are not smart enough to back off, well????

* Seeing the Whites of the Eyes – This is when the dog's pupils get really small and you can see "the whites of the eyes". It can also be called whale eye. This behavior is usually a last ditch effort to convince you that "I am really scared and don't want to bite you, but this is your last warning!" Need I say more?

❋ Rolling Over and Showing the Belly – This is the most submissive position a dog can take. The dog is basically saying "I am not worth hurting, look how worthless I am, please don't hurt me!" The only thing worse is showing the belly and peeing on himself as well. This dog is terrified...please stop.

A side note on the rolling over and showing belly and peeing. This is something that many puppies do normally, and unless you traumatize them, they will grow out of it. Either way, realize that you need to rethink what you are doing.

A common mistake here is assuming this dog is happy and wants his belly rubbed. While many dogs do immediately roll over and ask for belly rubs, this is totally different! This behavior is more like a wrestler or MMA fighter tapping out to stop the match. If you are paying attention and looking at all the behaviors the dog is giving you will know the difference!

There are a couple of other things I want to share in regards to body language and signals before we move on. The biggest misconception about dogs is that a wagging tail means a happy dog! This could not be further from the truth, and brings me to a critical lesson in the need to learn the language of dogs. You cannot take just one behavior and try to read a dog. You must look at the whole picture. You cannot look at just the tail, or ears, or the hair on the back. Just like people, different dogs are going to have slightly different ways to say the same or different things. For example, my dog Lexi completely hackles up (hair up all the way down her back) while she is playing with other dogs. It just goes to show that one signal is not reliable. Whereas, looking at all the signals together will give you a total picture to observe and make a judgment. A little tip for those wanting to hone their skills; you might consider going to a dog park without a dog and just sit and watch. Actually seeing dogs in action when you don't have to watch your own is a great way to observe and learn about dogs and their signals. And if you volunteer on a regular basis, your skills are going to improve, but that is no reason for not going the extra mile.

So why am I so passionate about this topic? Well that is easy. I don't want to see anyone who loves dogs and has decided to help a shelter, or their own dog, get hurt. The only way to reach that goal is education, and even with that, we are still dealing with an animal. Any animal, including a person, is unpredictable.

A final thought on safety in a shelter or at home…there is no shame in admitting you are in over your head. There are going to be issues and behaviors that you do not understand. There are going to be dogs at the shelter you just don't feel comfortable dealing with. Call a trainer for your dog at home and tell the kennel manger you don't feel comfortable when volunteering. The best trainers are those folks that admit when they need help or do not have an answer. The even better ones are those who ask for help or are willing to admit their own limits and are willing to refer to another. For your sake and the sake of the dogs you are and will be working with, only do what you feel comfortable doing, and never be afraid to ask for help. Learning never occurs in a vacuum and it is up to you to take this and other information and run with it. It serves to make you a better dog owner and a better shelter volunteer.

CONCLUSION

Writing this book has been a challenge and a pleasure all at the same time. As I read and edit it (for what seems the 150th time), I realize it is way more than a book on how to be a great shelter volunteer. It is really a book about dogs, dog training and the ability to relate to your dog without malice, over the top control or even dominance. I am very proud of the ideas here, and really hope that all the people that read this book rush out to their local shelter, sign up as a volunteer and make a difference. I also realize this book has the potential to help people inside their own home with their own dogs, leading to a happier home for everyone involved. Even at the time of writing this last chapter, I have no idea what the title of the book will be. It was originally to be titled "So You Want to Be a Shelter Volunteer", but in looking at the final product I think it covers way more than that.

I can only hope that you, the reader, agree. I ask you to take this information, share it, find someone to help or maybe even decide to go out and join the group of us that are lucky enough to work with dogs and their owners for a living. (Dog Trainer is really not accurate, since we are first and foremost people trainers!) Every author thinks, or at least hopes, that everything they write will be thought of as a "masterpiece"! I hold no such hopes. I know there are as many different ways to train a dog as there are types of dogs in the world. Rather, I hope you found a nugget or two in this book that you cannot wait to try. Thank you for supporting Keep it Simple Stupid (KISS) Dog Training and go out and make a difference with your own dog or others' dogs. In the end, it is all about saving more dogs and finding them their forever homes. I hope I have given you a few ideas to try along the way.

If you are interested in a live seminar on this information for your club or shelter, please contact KISS Dog training at www.kissdogtraining.com [http://www.kissdogtraining.com/] or find us on various social media outlets for more information on dogs and dog training! We are conveniently located in the Kansas City Metro!

Mike

Mike Deathe
CCPDT-KA